**Speaking your Mind:
Oral Presentation and Seminar Skills**

Series Editor: DR REBECCA STOTT

Other titles in the series:

Grammar and Writing
Rebecca Stott and Peter Chapman (Eds)

Writing with Style
Rebecca Stott and Simon Avery (Eds)

Making your Case: A Practical Guide to Essay Writing
Rebecca Stott, Anna Snaith and Rick Rylance (Eds)

Speaking your Mind: Oral Presentation and Seminar Skills

Edited by Rebecca Stott, Tory Young and Cordelia Bryan

Series Editor: Rebecca Stott

An imprint of **Pearson Education**

Harlow, England · London · New York · Reading, Massachusetts · San Francisco · Toronto · Don Mills, Ontario · Sydney
Tokyo · Singapore · Hong Kong · Seoul · Taipei · Cape Town · Madrid · Mexico City · Amsterdam · Munich · Paris · Milan

Pearson Education Limited
Edinburgh Gate
Harlow
Essex CM20 2JE
England

and Associated Companies throughout the world

Visit us on the World Wide Web at:
http://www.pearsoneduc.com

First published 2001

ISBN 0 582 38243 2

British Library Cataloguing-in-Publication Data
A catalogue record for this book is available from the British Library

10 9 8 7 6 5 4 3 2 1
04 03 02 01

Typeset by 35 in 10.5/12.5pt Janson Text
Printed and bound in Malaysia,LSP

CONTENTS

AUTHOR'S
ACKNOWLEDGEMENTS

This book and the other three books in the Speak–Write Series, *Grammar and Writing*, *Writing with Style*, and *Making your Case: A Practical Guide to Essay Writing*, have been three years in the making. They are the result of three years of research, teaching design and piloting undertaken by the Speak–Write Project, established by the English Department of Anglia Polytechnic University in Cambridge and funded by the Higher Education Funding Council for England through its Fund for the Development of Teaching and Learning. The Speak–Write Project was set up to respond to claims from members of English departments across the country that first-year undergraduates needed more intensive advanced writing and speaking courses at foundation level in order to perform more effectively in higher education.

Although the Speak–Write Project looked closely at freshman rhetoric and composition classes which have run successfully in the United States for decades, the Speak–Write designers and researchers concluded that there was a need in British higher education for innovative communication skills courses which were embedded in specific subject areas and not generic skills courses alone. These four books have been piloted, designed and adapted by and for lecturers and students working in English Literature departments and much of the material presented for analysis or rewriting or adaptation is of a literary kind. This said, the books have a much wider application and can be adapted for use by a range of cognate disciplines in the Humanities.

The Speak–Write books have drawn on the imaginations, time and work of many people. The editors and authors of individual books and chapters are acknowledged beneath the chapter and book titles. Many more people and institutions have contributed who remain invisible and I would like to thank as many of them individually here as possible: Tory Young, Editorial

Assistant, who saw the books through their final metamorphosis, tire-lessly and with great good humour and editorial skill; Ruth Maitland, the Speak–Write Project's Administrator, who held everything together; Rob Pope (Oxford Brookes University), Stephen Minta (York University), Val Purton (City College, Norwich), Morag Styles (Homerton College, Cambridge) and Katy Wales (Leeds University), the External Readers who assessed and advised on early drafts of the books; Paul Boyd, Richard James, Regine Hasseler, Shelby Bohland and Lucy Wood, the student editorial advis-ory group; Elizabeth Mann, Commissioning Editor at Longman, for her encouragement and enthusiasm for the Project in its early stages; staff and students of the English Department at Anglia Polytechnic University who have refined and shaped the books through giving continual feedback on aspects of teaching and learning; and my first-year students of 1999 in par-ticular for applying their creative minds to difficult editorial decisions.

Rebecca Stott, *Series Editor*

PUBLISHER'S ACKNOWLEDGEMENTS

We are grateful to the following for permission to reproduce copyright material:

Anglia Polytechnic University for sample 'criteria sheet for peer oral assessment' and 'sample practice presentation scenarios'; The Peters Fraser & Dunlop Group Limited on behalf of James Berry for the poem 'On an Afternoon train from Purley to Victoria' from *CHAIN OF DAYS* published by Oxford University Press © James Berry; BT for the advertising slogan *'IT'S GOOD TO TALK'* which is a registered trade mark in the United Kingdom of British Telecommunications plc; Channel 4 Television for a transcript from 'Booked' shown in December 1998; Guardian Newspapers Ltd for an extract from the article 'Members of the Jury' by Pat Bottle in *THE GUARDIAN* 27.6.91; Holmes and Marchant (Heinz public affairs) for Heinz Baby Foods advertisement, 1966; SmithKline Beecham plc for Eno's 'Fruit Salt' advertisement, 1890 and Unilever plc for Vim advertisement, 1935.

We have been unable to trace the copyright holders of the WRAC Officer advertisement and would appreciate any information which would enable us to do so.

INTRODUCTION

Rebecca Stott

Salman Rushdie once gave a lecture called 'Is Nothing Sacred?' in which he famously described literature as like a voice-room, a place where a number of conflicting voices discuss the world in which we live. Imagine, he said, that you wake up one morning in a large rambling house with all sorts of activities and conflicts and relationships going on all around you. You try to make sense of it and to find your way around it but you don't seem to make any progress until one day you find a little unimportant-looking room. In this room there are voices that seem to be whispering just to you:

> You recognise some of the voices, others are completely unknown to you. The voices are talking about the house, about everyone in it, about every-thing that is happening and has happened and should happen. Some of them speak exclusively in obscenities. Some are bitchy. Some are loving. Some are funny. Some are sad. The most interesting voices are all these things at once . . .

Then he asks the audience to imagine waking up one morning and finding that all the voice-rooms have disappeared. The voices they had heard talking about everything in every possible way are now silent.

> Now you remember: there is no way out of this house. Now this fact begins to seem unbearable. You look into the eyes of the people in the corridors – family, lovers, friends, colleagues, strangers, bullies, priests. You see the same thing in everybody's eyes. *How do we get out of here?* It becomes clear that the house is a prison. People begin to scream, and pound the walls. Men arrive with guns. The house begins to shake. You do not wake up. You are already awake. . . . Wherever in the world the little room of liter-ature has been closed, sooner or later the walls have come tumbling down.

(Rushdie 1990: 16)

Rushdie's lecture, delivered to an international audience of writers and intellectuals, and published so that it reached an even wider audience, was a powerful, and for him dangerous, defence of free speech in the wake of the violence and conflict which his book *The Satanic Verses* caused in 1989. Through the parable of the house with the voice-rooms, he argues that when totalitarian states impose extreme censorship upon their writers, when the voices in literature are not free to talk about everything in every possible way, life becomes unbearable for those living under that regime. Communities of people need to talk about the world in which they live and they need to be able to do it freely or their world will seem like a prison.

Rushdie was not the first to say that books are like conversations. Mikhail Bakhtin, a Russian intellectual who suffered both censorship and exile for his radical ideas under the Stalinist regime in the Soviet Union, said that novels were inherently 'polyphonic', meaning that they have many sounds or many voices. In some novels these many voices, all expressing slightly different ways of looking at the world, different beliefs and outlooks, continue to talk to each other and to disagree right the way through to the end of the novel, and we still feel that those debates and discussions continue after we have closed the book. This he called the dialogic novel (dialogue – two or more voices). In other novels the debates are all closed down by the end in favour of *one* dominant way of looking at the world. This he called the monologic novel (monologue – one voice). The first kind, which Bakhtin preferred, involves its readers in the dialogue, whereas the second kind of novel has a tendency to preach at its readers.

Talk is everywhere, then, even on the printed page. A British Telecom advertising campaign tells us that 'It's good to talk', but talk is not just good, it also is necessary, transformative, sometimes dangerous. 'Careless talk costs lives', the famous British war poster claimed. So much of what we do happens through talk, with ourselves, with our friends, with strangers. We come to understand new ideas by listening, talking and asking questions. Monologue is important as a way of receiving information, but we put that information to the test in dialogue. In universities students listen to a lecturer talking for a whole hour at a time, explaining nuclear physics or the poetic structures of Keats's odes, but it is in the seminar or the tutorial that those ideas are fully explored and tested out in dialogue with others. In families children may listen to parents explaining the rules of the game Monopoly, but it is only when they ask questions and then play the game with others that they can be said to know how to play. Dialogue and monologue are not as easy to separate as we may have thought. They are both parts of a complex process by which we change through learning new ideas and debating and testing them.

Just as there are hundreds of different ways in which we write to and for each other, there are hundreds of ways in which we talk. How do people learn or teach themselves to talk better? What are the skills of a good speaker?

How can they be acquired? Many books offer crash courses in better speaking or better conversation, but in this book we begin with the belief that there are no easy answers to these questions because they depend upon the context in which the talking is taking place. Dialogue-talk, such as in conversations, seminars and meetings, is different from, yet related to monologue-talk, which is what we do when we stand up and speak uninterrupted for a predetermined amount of time. Some people have excellent monologue skills but are hopeless in conversation because they do not like being interrupted and because they do not know how (or perhaps want) to interact with the audience. Others shine in the parry and thrust of a seminar but lose energy and direction when they face an audience that is not interrupting to ask questions or put other points of view.

Most effective speakers are flexible, able to adapt the manner of their speaking to the particular context. A good lecturer, for instance, will usually know what s/he wants to achieve in the hour, doesn't rush the audience, knows that they will get bored, may not understand, and may want to ask questions, but is able to anticipate those questions and adapt the lecture taking their needs into consideration. A good conversationalist or member of a seminar group knows when to speak and when to listen, asks questions, and is attentive to the shape of the conversation taking place. Much of what we do in conversation happens almost by instinct. After all, we have been learning how to converse since we first entered conversations before we even had speech – the baby turns its head towards the speaking face and makes its own responding mimicking noises from a few months old. Good dialogue is teamwork, with all the participants instinctively understanding the various roles they play as questioners, listeners and talkers.

So, if we are all already talking to others in a variety of different contexts every day and adapting instinctively to these different contexts, why did we set out to write another book about speaking skills? Well, we felt that the book we wanted to write had not yet been written. We did not want to write a book which claimed to do everything, improve our readers' skills in seminars, meetings, conversations, public speeches and marketing, but rather to look at the kind of talk we engage in at universities, which is primarily about persuading and arguing. As this book and indeed the series of which it is part are aimed at first-year undergraduates, we asked third-year undergraduates about what kind of help they needed in speaking in their first year at university. The answers fell into three groups. Students felt they needed help in:

- learning to argue more effectively
- thinking about how a seminar worked and advice on how to improve their skills as participants (dialogue)
- learning to be able to give a brief presentation to a small group which would be persuasive in form, concise and well-delivered (monologue).

Of course these three skills are equally important outside higher education, as many of the skills which employers say they look for in employees are derived from these three important areas. These specific aims, then, are what we have concentrated on in this book, but we also hope that by the time our readers have finished reading and using it, their ways of talking in many different forms and contexts will have been improved and stimulated.

We have structured the book around the three key aims. Chapter 1 begins with conversation, the kind of conversation in which all participants are actively engaged in discussion, conversation that is serious and potentially transformative. It then ends with the most formal kind of conversation, the seminar – formal because it is usually time-limited and led by a tutor or facilitator. As persuasive talk is one of the cornerstones of this book, we introduce rhetoric, the ancient art of persuasion, in Chapter 2. We argue here that rhetoric is not just of use to the politician seeking to manipulate words for political ends, but that these ancient arts have much to offer anyone seeking to present an argument to a contemporary audience, even in an informal context. As different communities and cultures have different traditions of arguing and persuading others, it is, of course, better to talk of contemporary 'rhetorics' than it is to talk just of rhetoric. Chapter 2 is about argument and the different roles that people take when they argue. This book aims to combine analysis of speaking and practice of speaking, and as a result each chapter has a different balance of analysis and practice. Chapter 3, for instance, on Shakespeare and Renaissance rhetoric, takes what has been taught in Chapter 2 about rhetoric and its influence through the centuries, and shows how it came to shape Shakespeare's plays in particular. All writing is a form of argument in many ways and much can be learned about the different positions taken up in a text through a working knowledge of rhetoric. Chapters 4 and 5, on the other hand, are much more practical and offer straightforward advice on how to prepare and deliver a short presentation which aims to make a case on a particular subject, using what has been taught earlier in the book on argument, rhetoric and dialogue.

How to use this book

We have structured the book very carefully and progressively and we will often be referring back to parts we have already covered and forward to items not yet dealt with. Broadly speaking then, we are advising you not just to *read*, but to *work through* the sequences of steps and examples from Chapters 1 to 6. Some of the activities will be more demanding (in terms of time and level of difficulty) than others. Most chapters have about ten to twelve activities to complete, each of which will enhance your understanding of the material in the chapter in different ways, and most activities can be adapted for either individuals or groups. However, there are a few which are group-only activities because they are based on discussion. We have provided enough activities in each chapter for readers to choose those which best suit their particular needs, interests and circumstances.

Reference

Rushdie, Salman (1990) *Is Nothing Sacred?*, Herbert Read Memorial Lecture. London: Granta.

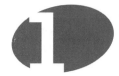

Conversations and seminars

Anna Snaith

I n this chapter we will look at how the conventions of conversation have changed through history and the numerous and varied forms that conversation takes in contemporary society from the TV chat show to the internet chat room and the chance conversation with a stranger on a train. We will introduce some of the ways linguists have analysed what happens when two or more people converse, the effect that gender has on group interaction, and how even the most casual conversations are full of unspoken conventions and expectations. Finally we will examine the seminar as the most formal kind of conversation, formal because it is usually time-limited and involves a leader or chairperson.

Conversation

The word 'conversation' comes from the Old French word 'converser' ('con' means 'together'), which means 'to keep company with', and this implicit meaning is important – conversation is keeping company through words. It is at the heart of social interaction. It is always done with others, even if those others are imaginary people inside your own head. Another word we use to describe conversation is 'dialogue', which comes from the Greek word 'dialogos', a word made up of two parts: 'dia', which means 'between two', and 'logos', which means 'word'. Dialogue then means the speaking that passes backwards and forwards between two or more people.

Conversation is vital to our development and fulfilment as human beings. Relationships are formed and developed through talk, in groups of two or more. Conversations are not necessarily about anything very important.

Sometimes the act of talking and communicating is what matters, rather than the content of the speech. Think of the number of conversations that you have on any given day. They are all different, serve different purposes and occur in different contexts. Some may be telephone or e-mail conversations, others may be face-to-face. On a given morning, you will most likely find yourself in a series of different conversations or discussions: a chat with a partner or flatmate over breakfast about the day ahead, a brief interchange with the postperson or the bus conductor, a group discussion meeting at work, or a seminar group at college, a conversation with a friend or colleague over lunch. Sometimes conversations go smoothly and we come away feeling that we have successfully conveyed certain information, that we have become closer to someone or found out more about them. In the Canadian writer Carol Shield's novel *Larry's Party* (1998), the narrator describes the protagonist Larry Weller's ongoing conversation with his colleague in the florists where he works:

> He and Viv talk all day long. They've been talking for twelve years, an unceasing, seamless conversation . . . Larry and Viv hold it steady and fluid with their voices, his, hers – talking, talking, all day the two of them talking.

> (Shields 1998: 64)

Larry and Viv's conversations flow naturally and easily. On the other hand, conversation can leave us feeling uneasy or worried that we have offended someone. We may have said too much, or too little, been too direct or fudged around an issue. We may have been with a larger group and felt we couldn't get a word in, or feel we dominated the conversation and bored everyone. Analysing how conversation works can help us to be more in control of group-speaking situations. We can be aware of when a conversation or discussion is taking a course we would rather it didn't take. We can think more about the context or body language of our conversations. We can improve or alter our conversational style in certain situations. Start listening to yourself and analyse your own conversations.

ACTIVITY 1:

Keep a record of memorable conversations you have had over the course of a particular day. At the end of the day write up a short report reflecting upon your experience. Which conversational settings made you feel comfortable or uncomfortable? What roles do you tend to take in conversations? Do these roles change depending upon the people you are talking with? How would you describe your own conversational style? What are you good at or less good at? What makes a good conversation in your view?

Conversation in history

Studying conversation in different cultures at different historical moments can tell us much about those societies: where, when and why people converse, and what they talk about. There are countries and societies in which people are not allowed to converse freely due to dictatorial governments. There are communities in which people choose *not* to converse. Some members of the Amish community in the United States, for example, use a silent discourse, communicating through signs, symbols and action rather than words. They wish to reach a higher level of spirituality by avoiding the ambiguities and conflicts potentially caused by language and conversation. As difficult as it is to generalise about conversational trends in history, let us look at a few culturally and historically distinct ways of conversing.

Socrates, a Greek philosopher of the fifth century BC, used conversation and dialogue to explore philosophical ideas. He introduced the idea that people cannot be intelligent on their own but that they need someone else to stimulate them. Two or more people talking together can discover more truth than they could do individually. We know about Socrates from the writings of one of his students, Plato, who presents him as a master of the art of speaking. Rather than lecturing, however, Socrates used conversation and discussion to explore ideas on right and wrong, happiness, and existence. This is referred to as the Socratic method, and consisted of Socrates asking his students a series of questions (to which he professed not to know the answer) in order to arrive at a conclusion. Plato's *Dialogues* and *Symposium* are evidence of how conversation was used in this context to educate and illuminate. Talk was restricted to 'serious' matters; gossip was not permitted.

In medieval Europe the tradition of courtly love was another context in which conversation was central, but used for rather a different purpose. Originating in eleventh-century France, this new concept of love consisted of a male lover courting a woman by acting as her servant, worshipping at the altar of his lady love. These relationships were both marital and extramarital, but emphasised the secret, private nature of the love. The meetings of courtly lovers were based around conversations on love and loyalty. These conversations were highly formalised and made use of recognisable figures of speech and conventions.

The rise of the salon and the coffee-house provides a context for a different kind of conversation, one that is much less ritualised than that of Socrates or the tradition of courtly love. Seventeenth-century France saw the burgeoning of the salon: a weekly meeting of between one and two dozen men and women held in someone's home, usually presided over by a woman with a talent for drawing out the best talk in the guests who had been invited not because they were rich but because they had interesting things to say. Many of the guests were writers, interested in the salon as a forum for conversation on interesting topics. Unlike a party, the salons were regular meetings in which men and women talked together and produced epigrams, verse, eulogies, music, games and maxims as well as conversation. Katherine Philips, who started a salon in London in the middle of the seventeenth century, described her salon as 'a Society of Friendship to which male and female members were admitted, and in which poetry, religion and the human heart were to form the subjects of discussion' (Zeldin 1998: 37). This salon had much in common with the meetings of the Bloomsbury Group, a group of writers and artists who met in a house at 46 Gordon Square, Bloomsbury, London, on Thursday evenings at the beginning of the twentieth century.

In eighteenth-century England conversation generally became more informal. Previously it had often been a public means of displaying one's learning, and therefore made use of rhetoric, or the art of persuasion. The first coffee-house opened in 1652 and by the eighteenth century the hundreds of coffee-houses in London provided a place where men could go to discuss art, literature, politics and economics. A penny admission meant the chance to converse on serious and trivial matters, drink coffee and read the newspaper. Many Londoners spent large amounts of time in the coffee-houses. This public place of discussion and conversation marked the rise of the bourgeoisie, giving the new middle class opportunities to mix with the aristocracy in the coffee-houses.

Class is a crucial factor in the history of conversation. In 1908 a doctor wrote that she doubted whether 'any real conversation between members of two classes is possible. All conversations with my patients and their friends have been of an exceedingly one-sided character . . . in some cases I talked, and in some cases they did, but we never took anything like equal parts' (Zeldin 1998: 39). Although conversation can be effective in establishing equality and tolerance between individuals or groups, perceived inequalities between speakers can be a barrier to communication. Social factors such as gender, race and class affect how people perceive one another, and hence how they converse.

In African-American culture the porch is an important place of conversation. People (usually men) gather on the porch of one of their homes, or of the local store, to tell stories and to converse about daily events. Here, the location of conversation is important – the porch is a liminal space between inside and outside, public and private. The porch is both a public stage and a private interior. Conversation is then both entertainment and leisure. African-American writer and anthropologist Zora Neale Hurston writes about the porch in her novel *Their Eyes Were Watching God*. In the town of Eatonville, Florida, the porch is the place where black folklore is preserved through story-telling and where the town's values and traditions are maintained through conversation. The female protagonist is initially talked *about*, excluded from the porch, and the novel is about her eventual participation in the porch talk. This is an excerpt from the opening of the novel:

> It was the time for sitting on porches beside the road. It was the time to hear things and talk . . . They passed nations through their mouths. They sat in judgement.

> (Hurston 1986: 3–4)

Varieties of conversation

Late twentieth-century Western culture has seen the proliferation of types of conversation. For many people, the dinner table is no longer the focus for conversations with family and friends. New formats for conversation have arisen due to the rise of media and communication technology. Computer networks operate 'chat rooms' where subscribers can have virtual conversations with each other. As with telephone conversation, the talking partners cannot see each other, and so body language becomes irrelevant, but the rise of chat rooms has raised the possibility of the creation of new identities through conversation. When conversing with strangers whom one will most likely never meet, one can play with identity, inventing a new name, occupation, or switching gender.

A media phenomenon centred around conversation is the talk show. Shows such as *The Oprah Winfrey Show* and *Rikki Lake* enjoyed enormous popularity in the 1990s. In 1993 *The Oprah Winfrey Show* attracted fifteen million viewers per show, more than any news programme or soap opera. As the name suggests, the talk show works on the principle of the talking cure. The host facilitates discussion of a designated topic by interviewing guests, seeking the advice of an 'expert', and encouraging audience participation in the discussion. The conversation is extended beyond the stage. Talk shows tap into the late twentieth-century interest in people's private, psychological, emotional and sexual lives, the more sensational the better! The sets of talk shows often look like living rooms to heighten the idea that the audience is voyeuristically listening in on a private conversation. Much breakfast TV follows this line – with guests and presenters lounging on settees. Like celebrity chat shows (e.g. *Mrs Merton, Late Night With David Letterman*), these are meant to look like natural conversations rather than staged interviews.

Other types of discussion groups are a twentieth-century phenomenon. Book groups, incredibly popular in North America and increasingly so in Britain, consist of groups of people who meet monthly or fortnightly in someone's home to discuss a novel. Church prayer groups meet to discuss prayer and religion in much the same way. These conversational formats are for educational as well as social or leisure purposes.

Analysing conversation

Conversation analysis is important in sociology, psychology, linguistics and anthropology. Conversation tells us about how people interact with each other in different cultures, communities and across gender lines. Our own conversation tells us about ourselves: what are our priorities, values, feelings etc. It is therefore important to analyse private speech, or informal conversation, as well as looking at public speaking and formal presentations. This kind of speech, too, follows patterns and conventions. Conversation analysts have a method for transcribing conversations which allows them to record tone, pitch, overlapping voices, pauses and repetition, as well as the words themselves.

When conversing, most people follow certain assumed principles: that having entered into a conversation they will not obstruct its flow, that they will speak truthfully and clearly, and that they follow the principle of politeness (to varying degrees!). If you think back over your recent casual conversations you will probably find that most of them followed these principles. Imagine if we met a friend in the street and asked how they were and they replied 'Asparagus', we would feel they had breached the conventions of conversation. (Either that or that we were in a surrealist play!) We would feel the friend was obstructing the flow of conversation, since we expected a range of responses such as 'Fine', 'Pretty awful', 'OK' or 'Great'. Imagine a TV interview that went like this:

Interviewer: We are very privileged to have with us today a farmer from Hampshire, Mr John Jones, who has just beaten the world record for growing the biggest watermelon. How do you feel about breaking a World Record, Mr Jones?

JJ: I couldn't care less.

I: Was it you who reported the watermelon?

JJ: No.

I: Who was it then?

JJ: Don't know.

I: Have you been celebrating?

JJ: Course not.

Going through life obstructing conversation like Mr Jones will probably mean opportunities for conversation become few and far between! Of course there are people who converse in this way, and some of us may have spent part or all of our teenage years speaking to our parents like this. Think of Kevin the Teenager on the TV comedy show *Harry Enfield*.

Conversation is not just about words. Part of conversation is non-verbal, encompassing body language and gestures. If a friend arrives at your door and you greet him/her with 'Hello, great to see you. Do come in and make yourself at home', but you are standing blocking the doorway with your arms crossed, the *metamessage* (the sum total of content, context and body language) may be that the visitor is unwelcome. Another way of saying this is that the host has not *framed* the meaning appropriately. Misunderstanding in conversation is often the result of a discrepancy between the words and the frame of those words. We can signal what kind of occasion the conversation is and what we want to convey by tone, pitch, intonation, body language and expression, as well as through the language itself. If we are offering an apology in a raised voice, or are consoling an ill friend in an accusatory tone, the recipient is likely to be confused and feel s/he is receiving mixed signals. Conversation is often accompanied by gestures: some people use hand and head gestures more than others. These can be used to effect, or can be distracting or a sign of nervousness. Gestures can be *iconic* (mimic what they refer to, for example the size of some object) or by convention stand for a certain meaning (e.g. a nod of the head means affirmation). Eye contact is another essential part of the non-verbal aspect of conversation. People assume that you will make eye contact during conversation. Avoiding doing so can signal deceit, embarrassment or unease with the situation. It could also signal to the speaker that you are not listening or are not interested.

As we engage people in conversation, we are constantly assessing the conversation and the other person's conversational style. Are they quiet, and therefore do we need to initiate conversation? Are they talkative, and so do we need to assert ourselves into the conversation? Are they always looking for affirmation? Some miscommunication can be solved, therefore, by being aware of other people's or cultures' styles of conversation. As conversationalists, however, we need to be aware of the signals, the metamessages that we are sending. Other cultures may generally speak more loudly, may be more or less forthright in conversation, may have different intonation (e.g. their voice may go up at the end of sentences). Different groups of people will have different conversational styles.

Imagine the following example. Josh takes his new boyfriend, Alex, to meet his family for the first time. Alex is shocked at the pitch of the conversation. Members of Josh's family seem to be shouting angrily at one another the whole evening. Alex feels intimidated, as though he's intruding on an intimate family row. However, this is just the style of conversation in that family. Alex learns to raise the pitch and intensity of his voice when visiting Josh's family.

Conversation is based on give and take. Mr Jones in the earlier example was not doing any giving. This may be the norm for certain types of conversation, for example a suspect being interviewed by a policeperson, or a hostage being interrogated by a terrorist, but in everyday conversation we can expect co-operation from our talking partner. Conversation analysts speak of *adjacency pairs*, which consist of a *first pair part* and a *second pair part*. These pairs consist of an utterance and a response. They could be a question and answer, or a statement and a response. For example:

> 1: How are you?
> 2: Very well thank you.
>
> 1: This weather is awful.
> 2: Yes, it's unusually rainy for July.

Blocks of conversation can be analysed as a series of *turn-taking*. This can flow naturally, or can be rather awkward. There are those people who never give you a turn, or those people who don't take their turn and either cut short the conversation or make you do all the talking. Other people like to talk about themselves and never ask questions of the other person. We have certain ways of letting our talking partner know we want to speak. These are called *turn-suppressing cues* (letting the speaker know s/he should give up the turn), such as a raised hand or urgent nods or turning towards someone else, or *turn-claiming cues* (indicating that you want to speak). Another way which we often use is interruption, or speaking over the speaker. This can avoid awkward pauses, or it can be competitive and mean that the recipient does not actually listen to what the speaker is trying to say. *Pre-emptive turn completion* occurs when we complete the speaker's sentence.

Opening and closing

Much of conversation is about convention. Indeed, conversation is important in the study of how society operates according to sets of rules. A lot of conversations are entirely predictable, what we call *small talk*. This does not mean they serve no purpose: verbal interaction itself is the goal here rather than communication of information or emotion. We are so accustomed, for example, to hearing 'OK', 'Fine' or 'Alright' when we ask someone how they are, that if they reply 'Incredible!' we are likely to hesitate, or comment on their response. The parts of a conversation that are most likely to be predictable and conventional are the opening and closing sections. We rarely come up to someone and say, 'My grandmother died yesterday' or 'What do you think about abortion?' We need time to ease into the conversation. In service encounters (e.g. making an appointment with a doctor, buying a train ticket) we may dispense with such openings and start the conversation with 'I have a pain in my foot' or 'A single ticket to Nottingham please'. The openings of non-service encounters, however, usually start with some kind of small talk (in Britain, notoriously about the weather), particularly if the speakers are strangers to each other. Or they might begin with a pseudo-apology such as 'Sorry to trouble you but . . .' or 'I don't mean to bother you but . . .'.

Endings of conversations (*terminal exchange*) also follow familiar patterns. For example:

> 1: Goodbye
> 2: Bye
>
> 1: Nice to talk to you.
> 2: Yes, take care.

Usually conversations are ended when one speaker introduces a topic which is *closing implicative*: for example, 'I'd better go now. I've got to meet my daughter in fifteen minutes' or 'Well, I hope I can see you again soon'. Such phrases signal the desire to close the conversation.

The language of conversation

There are certain linguistic structures which are commonly found in conversation. One of these is *elliptical grammatical forms* (incomplete sentences). This is because conversation is often informal and also because it is verbal rather than written. Unlike sending a letter or writing an essay, in conversation we can go back and fill in the gaps. Also, conversation often relies on common or shared knowledge so not everything needs to be fully spelt out, particularly something which has just been referred to. For example:

> 1: Not all the women who went on the demo were single mothers.
> 2: Most were though.

Instead of repeating 'Most were single mothers though', Speaker 2 uses an elliptical form. A further example would be:

> 1: Drink?
> 2: Beer please.

Speaker 1 does not need to say 'Would you like a drink?' in the informal situation, and Speaker 2 leaves out 'Yes, I would like . . .' for the same reason.

Similarly, most casual conversation uses *contractions* (e.g. it's, doesn't) for expediency. Many *deictic* words (pointing words, e.g. this, that, here) occur in conversation because of this idea of shared knowledge. Deictic words are also part of the cohesion which speakers create in their conversations. To some degree, conversations need to flow. If every adjacency pair introduced a totally new topic, the speakers would more than likely come away feeling they had not really discussed anything. Cohesion is also created through *anaphoric reference* (referring back to earlier material). Look at the following:

> 1: Would you like one of these cakes?
> 2: Which ones are they?
>
> 1: They're from that party Joseph had last week.
> 2: The one in that old house?

Look for the deictic and anaphoric references even in this short excerpt from a conversation. Immediately we can see the amount of information which the two speakers share and take for granted.

Casual conversation is full of forms which we do not find in written English. Listen to one of your conversations for the number of *filler* and *reinforcer words* such as 'like', 'umm', 'well', 'sort of', 'yup', or 'right'. In conversation we have to think as we speak, hence the pauses, as well as the filler words, which buy us time as we construct our sentences. Filler words also cushion what we say. If we have to tell someone something unpleasant or embarrassing we often use more filler words. Reinforcer words reassure the speaker that we are listening and that we agree with or understand what s/he is saying. The speaker often asks for such affirmation with phrases like 'Do you know what I mean?'

Repetition of words and phrases is often found in casual conversation. Again, this is to buy time, but also to ensure effective communication. When we read, we often go back over the same sentence, but with conversation this is not an option.

Listening and asking questions

Holding effective conversations is not just about speaking. Being an active listener is essential to fulfilling interaction. Breakdowns in communication, particularly in intimate relationships, are often due to one party feeling that they are not being heard, that there is no one to whom they can express themselves. Good listeners let the speaker know that they are listening – they are active and take part in the conversation by nodding, intervening with 'yes' or 'hmm', or asking questions. This is called *back-channel behaviour*. This shows that the listener has understood and processed what has been said. We need to make sure we actually hear what people say, rather than second-guessing what we think they are saying. Active listeners can draw a speaker out, asking open rather than closed questions (closed questions have yes or no answers and shut down communication lines).

Many problems with understanding what has been said occur because we don't focus completely on the speaker. We may be more concerned about how we might respond or we might be distracted by other thoughts. An excellent way of ensuring that you have understood the speaker is to paraphrase or summarise their comments in your own mind before you respond. Then if you're still not quite clear you will find it easier to formulate a question to help you understand better.

Good speakers usually give signposts to indicate the main structure of their points. These are usually clue words such as 'firstly', 'next', 'finally' or 'on the other hand'. Sometimes the signals come in sentences such as 'There are three ways . . .' or 'I will present four reasons . . .'. These let you know what is coming. Usually the signposts are emphasised by the speaker's tone of voice, inflection, body language and facial expression.

Active listening requires us to paraphrase and summarise and we do this by looking for key words and phrases, analogies and metaphors that make sense to us, as we listen. Sometimes we need to stop the speaker and ask questions like, 'So, what you are saying is . . . ?' Reflecting your own summary back to the speaker like this gives you a chance to test out whether you have understood and gives the speaker a chance to correct or adjust your understanding and clear up any misconceptions or questions you might have.

ACTIVITY 2:

You work for a local radio station and to coincide with the beginning of the school year your employer has asked you to run a five-minute feature on local residents' memories of their first day at school. Script a number of questions which you think will stimulate people to relate interesting stories and try these out on people who have been to local schools (there should be a mixture of people of different ages, backgrounds, genders etc.). If you have access to recording equipment you may use this, or alternatively take notes of people's responses to your questions. Write up the material into a five-minute feature in which you include a brief introduction and extracts from interviews with at least two people.

Write a short report analysing the process of making the feature and assessing the final feature itself. How effective were the questions you chose? How effective were your respondents in their recounting of their memories? How did you manage the interviewing so as to produce the best possible material?

ACTIVITY 3:

If you are working in groups, choose one person in the group who is prepared to answer questions and choose a subject which he or she feels happy to talk about. It might be a favourite book, or a hobby or interest. You have five minutes to find out as much as possible about this subject and the person's involvement and interest in it. The appointed person should only answer the questions asked, but can continue until they feel they have answered the question. Appoint an observer to keep notes. Which questions produced the most information? What kind of information did certain kinds of questions produce? What were the most unusual and interesting questions? Discuss the outcomes and write them up as a short report. If you are working alone, script an imaginary conversation of the kind described above in which you interview someone well known to you.

Gender and conversation

If we are looking at the ways in which conversation has changed historically, we need to look at gender and conversation. Women were not allowed into Socrates' discussion groups or the eighteenth-century coffee-houses, and the porch in African-American communities was dominated by male speech. Women's experience of conversation, therefore, is historically and socially different from that of men. Until the women's movement began in the mid-nineteenth century, women had restricted access to public places and were excluded from debate on and participation in public life. They were excluded from political life as their main role was thought to be in the home, as mothers and carers. It was therefore assumed that women's conversations were about domestic issues. Like the Victorian adage that children should be 'seen and not heard' (i.e. not take part in adult conversation), women were often silenced from talking about certain 'serious' issues. Women were expected to 'know their place' and not try and converse with men about 'male' issues such as politics or economics.

This has meant that women have been, and still are, associated with idle chatter and gossip, whereas men are thought to conduct conversations on serious matters. Henry David Thoreau, a nineteenth-century American writer, once criticised what he saw as the old-boy networks of power in Britain, a place where, he claimed, important political decisions were made at dinner tables, after the women had left the table: 'The government of the world I live in was not framed, like that of Britain, in after-dinner conversations over the wine' (Thoreau 1999: xx). Women's conversation is conventionally linked to the home, the domestic realm, people's daily lives and emotions, just as women themselves have historically been trapped in the private sphere.

These kinds of stereotypes still persist today. During the 1998 Football World Cup a TV advertisement featured a man engrossed in the football while a woman, his wife or partner, used the hour and a half to chatter on the phone to a female friend. The assumption here that football is for men, and chattering on the phone is for women, is evidence of the deep-rootedness of sexist stereotypes about how women converse and what they converse about.

Gender and conversation is a contentious issue amongst linguists and psychologists. Linguist Deborah Tannen, author of best-selling *You Just Don't Understand: Women and Men in Conversation* (1992), argues that men and women do talk differently, not for any essentialist or innate reasons, but because they are socialised differently. Tannen argues that a male/female conversation is a cross-cultural exchange and that men and women need, therefore, to understand how the other sex converses, so they can avoid miscommunication and breakdown of relationships. Tannen argues that in general women converse for the sake of communication, to connect with another person, to feel closer, whereas men view conversation as a means of conveying information, and so tend to be more direct, often hurting their female partner. She distinguishes between women's 'rapport-talk' and men's 'report-talk'. Women, she claims, tend to want to establish a rapport with someone, usually through private conversation, and men use conversation to report or convey information, generally in a more public or larger group situation. Women often feel men don't talk enough, or that male conversation can sometimes be lecturing, whereas men feel women nag them and do not say what they mean. 'Women speak and hear a language of connection and intimacy, while men speak and hear a language of status and independence' (Tannen 1992: 42).

Tannen also analyses gossip, perhaps the most commonly used synonym for women's conversation. Used pejoratively, the term implies that women talk too much about private matters. The late twentieth-century fascination with talk shows and fly-on-the-wall documentaries ties in with the notion of gossip – a fascination with the intimate details of people's private lives. Not surprisingly these genres of TV show are seen as 'female'. Gossip has been reclaimed by some feminists, including Tannen, as being necessary in creating and bonding friendships. The sense of shared knowledge or opinions about a third party cements relationships, but of course it also creates exclusivity and is a form of social control. Gossiping is a way of regulating values and behaviour; deviance from those norms is the subject of gossip. Gossiping is a way of informing someone else about what you find acceptable. What role does gossip play in your life? Is it a positive or a negative one?

The debate about gender and conversation will no doubt continue. The best-selling status of Tannen's study and the corroboration she constantly receives for her ideas suggest that at least some men and women do converse for different reasons at different times, but we need to avoid being prescriptive: this can lead to the perpetuation of sexist assumptions. Pay attention to your own conversations with the opposite sex: what is your opinion on gender and conversation?

Literary conversations

Most works of fiction make extensive use of conversation. Reporting indirectly or transcribing verbatim what characters say to each other serves several purposes in a novel or short story. To begin with, conversation brings a book to life. As readers, we are drawn into the story by reading characters' actual speech, rather than relying solely on a narrator's report. Having said this, the lack of conversation in a novel (i.e. the use of only a narrator's or single character's point of view) has its purposes, such as emphasising the psychology of one particular person. Conversation is an expedient way for a writer to create setting, character and atmosphere. From reading a few lines of conversation we can often have a rough idea of the historical and geographical setting of the book. The characters may speak with a particular dialect, for example, as in the novels of Scottish writer James Kelman. If this is portrayed through transcribed conversations, the writer has immediately alerted the reader to this aspect of place and character in the novel. A few lines of conversation can also reveal enormous amounts about the character. Rather than have a narrator describe a character, they can reveal themselves through speech.

In *Emma* by Jane Austen, for example, we learn about Emma's character through her conversation at a picnic on Box Hill. Austen is famous for how astutely and realistically, but yet subtly, she uses conversation for characterisation. In this scene, the problem, for Emma, is a lack of conversation. In trying to liven up the party, Emma asks the guests to tell her what they are thinking about. Initially Austen's narrator describes the answers: 'Some laughed, and answered good-humouredly. Miss Bates said a great deal; Mrs Elton swelled at the idea of Miss Woodhouse's presiding; Mr Knightley's answer was the most distinct.' Next, however, Emma asks everyone to entertain her with 'one thing very clever . . . two things moderately clever – or three things very dull indeed' (Austen 1985: 364). This is the conversation which follows:

> 'Oh! very well,' exclaimed Miss Bates, 'then I need not be uneasy. "Three things very dull indeed." That will just do for me, you know. I shall be sure to say three dull things as soon as ever I open my mouth, shan't I? – (looking round with the most good-humoured dependence on every body's assent) – Do not you all think I shall?'

Emma could not resist.

'Ah! ma'am, but there may be a difficulty. Pardon me – but you will be limited as to number – only three at once.'

Miss Bates, deceived by the mock ceremony of her manner, did not immediately catch her meaning; but, when it burst on her, it could not anger, though a slight blush showed that it could pain her.

'Ah! – well – to be sure. Yes, I see what she means, (turning to Mr Knightley,) and I will try to hold my tongue. I must make myself very disagreeable, or she would not have said such a thing to an old friend.'

(Austen 1985: 363–4)

Mr Knightley chastises Emma for her cruel words, and her repentance and grief at her thoughtlessness mark a turning point in the novel. This conversation is a crucial moment in Emma's gradual progression towards maturity and insight. Notice that Austen's narrator is still present in the scene above, providing extra information and description, but Emma's important comment to Miss Bates, and the latter's response, are presented verbatim. Through the characters' own words we see Emma's pride emerging from the sarcasm and pomposity in her voice, and we see Miss Bates's shock in her hesitation. Miss Bates turns to speak to Mr Knightley, as she cannot face Emma, and this is signalled by the narrator.

In plays, of course, the entire text is made up of conversation, unless the play is a monologue, or consists of soliloquies. Harold Pinter, a twentieth-century British playwright, is an extremely skilled writer of dialogue. He manages to write dialogue which sounds realistic and everyday, but also carries surreal, sinister and/or menacing undertones. He is also famous for the strategic use of the pause. In the following excerpt from his sketch called 'The Applicant', however, it is his use of interruption, rather than pauses, which is important. In the scene, an interviewee (Lamb) is being subjected to electric shock treatment, and the conversation creates Lamb's sense of panic, confusion and loss of control.

Piffs: Would you say you were an excitable person?
Lamb: Not – not unduly, no. Of course, I –
Piffs: Would you say you were a moody person?
Lamb: Moody? No, I wouldn't say I was moody – well, sometimes occasionally I –
Piffs: Do you ever get fits of depression?
Lamb: Well, I wouldn't call them depression exactly –
Piffs: Do you often do things you regret in the morning?
Lamb: Regret? Things I regret? Well, it depends what you mean by often, really – I mean when you say often –
Piffs: Are you often puzzled by women?
Lamb: Women?

Piffs: Men.
Lamb: Men? Well, I was just going to answer the question about women –
Piffs: Do you often feel puzzled?
Lamb: Puzzled?
Piffs: By women.
Lamb: Women?
Piffs: Men.
Lamb: Oh, now just a minute, I . . . Look, do you want separate answers or a joint answer?

(Pinter 1991: 226–7)

Lamb is not in control of the situation, or the conversation. He is only allowed to finish one sentence in this excerpt and the barrage of questions creates the tension which leads up to his electric shock treatment.

ACTIVITY 4:

Read this conversation out loud several times playing the voices of the two characters, paying particular attention to the length of the pauses and the tone and intonations of the speakers and trying to draw out the comedy of the situation as fully as you can. If you are working in groups, appoint two people to play these parts whilst the rest of the group directs the dialogue and action, again paying particular attention to the length of the pauses and the tone and intonation of the speakers. Write up a short report on Pinter's handling of this dramatic conversation and the different ways in which it could be directed. Include your ideas about body language and stage directions.

Seminars

This book is concerned with formal conversation. It sets out to help you improve your skills and understanding of the kinds of conversations which are formal and involve critical thinking and skills in argument and persuasion. However, even narrowing down conversation to the kinds of interactions people have in the university environment leaves us with a great deal of variety. The following are all kinds of speech acts that you are likely to be involved in at university:

- discussion group work – brainstorming
- problem-solving
- presenting a summary of someone else's point of view or theory
- chairing a small group
- explaining a theory to a group of non-specialists

- asking questions of a speaker or lecturer
- explaining the context to an issue or series of issues
- summarising conclusions reached by a group
- interviewing.

ACTIVITY 5:

Many of these skills are 'transferable' to the workplace. Identify the kinds of speech activities you will be required to do if you become either a teacher or a lawyer or involved in local politics. How many of these are skills that you are likely to have practised at university?

Now we need to think about discussion in groups, whether in seminars at a university, planning meetings at work, or the weekly meeting of an interest group. Let's focus for now on the seminar format. Students have mixed reactions to seminars (and so do tutors). They can be terrifying experiences for the quiet student who is afraid s/he will be picked on, or they can be platforms for the overconfident student who wants to show off his/her knowledge, or they can be mutually beneficial, illuminating and inspirational: times to share ideas, opinions and knowledge. The word seminar comes from the word 'seed', implying that the seminar is a place where ideas are planted like seeds, to grow and develop through discussion.

Analysing seminars

The following is an experienced tutor's opinion of what makes a good seminar.

I have been teaching for ten years now and in three different universities. Before that I attended a university in which the seminar was regarded as the centre of the educational process. Seminars were always two hours long and although tutors had a variety of different methods for shaping the seminars, students usually were in total agreement about what made a good seminar, and always knew when they had had one. I admit I've never liked tutorials as much as I like seminars. This is because I enjoy the greater range of ideas and opinions produced by a larger group and the sense of excitement, the sense that 'almost anything could happen'.

Over the years I can remember a number of seminars which were for various reasons quite inspirational. These were occasions in which suddenly we all as a group found ourselves in uncharted territory: a seminar based on an autobiography which described Edmund Gosse's extreme religious upbringing in which we discovered that over half the group had been raised in similar ways; a seminar on Keats's Odes in which the tutor kept us talking for two hours about just four lines of one ode; a seminar on gothic literature in which two students gave an opening presentation on why women wrote gothic novels which was so provocative that the discussion which followed did not stop until the two hours was up and needed no tutor intervention. Many of the most exciting seminars are those which cannot be predicted. I always think there is a little magic involved in the seminar – a kind of alchemy. You bring together a number of different people from different backgrounds and with different opinions and views and you give them something to discuss and some difficult questions and when it works there's a kind of transformation. Nobody leaves the room the same person they were when they came in.

These days I try to ensure variety in my seminars by changing the way we do things in discussion with the group. Some weeks we break up into smaller groups, other weeks we stay together for the full two hours, sometimes I ask people to start off the discussion with a few opening remarks, other times I ask everyone to bring along their 'most original idea' about the book we are discussing and write it up on the board for the others to discuss. The combination of full group and small group discussions means that those who are shy have more opportunities to talk. Sometimes people who are silent in the larger group really perform well in the smaller group discussions and as a tutor it is satisfying to watch people's speaking skills develop in interesting ways. The worst kind of seminars are those which have no energy, no edge to them. I tend to be able to tell quite quickly when this is the case from the way the students are sitting, by the lack of books and notes on the table, from the lack of eye contact. Everyone seems flat or tired or uninterested. This can often be a challenge for me to inject some enthusiasm or energy into the group but sometimes nothing works. People don't respond to questions with any enthusiasm. This is not usually because the material is boring but because the students are underprepared for some reason or other. Seminars like this can be like trying to push a large rock up a steep hill. The seminar has failed because the students have not shown a collective responsibility for the success of the seminar.

If I were asked to list the ingredients of a good seminar I would say:

- a clear set of aims and objectives agreed at the beginning
- not too large a group (thirteen to eighteen people maximum)
- enthusiastic, relaxed and well-prepared participants
- a good mix of opinions and people prepared to defend them
- interesting material to discuss
- good questions to consider
- a good mix of people who take different roles in the seminar: questioners, summarisers, those who develop other people's ideas, those who are prepared to be controversial, and enthusiastic listeners
- a tutor who guides the argument, sets the context and keeps asking questions but is not too dominant
- regular summaries of where the discussion has been and where it might head
- a certain level of seriousness broken up occasionally by good humour!

Collective responsibility and awareness of group dynamics

What makes the tutor's job so interesting is that no two seminars are ever the same: the dynamic of the group, the subject/text under discussion, the time of the meeting will all affect the discussion. Not every seminar will set the world on fire, but by being self-conscious about how your seminars are going you can find them much more fulfilling. By thinking as a group about how your seminar is progressing and by being attentive to the nature of your discussions, you will find that things can be changed and improved to make the experience more beneficial. This can be achieved in a democratic way through the participation of all the group members.

Mutual respect and interest

Everyone should feel comfortable in the seminar situation. People cannot express their ideas if they feel intimidated or alienated. Make sure you know everyone's name and everyone knows your name. Having each group member introduce themselves at the beginning of the semester breaks the ice, lets everyone speak once and means that you can address people by their name. Make sure your tutor *is* facilitating and that no one is being embarrassed or picked on, or the discussion will freeze up for everyone. The goal here is a supportive atmosphere, but one which does not degenerate into a free-for-all. Be aware of how you are functioning within the discussion: avoid nitpicking, attacking others' ideas, interrupting and whispering while others are speaking.

Good physical conditions

Seating arrangements are very important in any group discussion, as they can denote power and hierarchy. Most people find that sitting in a circle which includes the tutor works best, since separating the tutor off from rows of students invokes a lecture format and inhibits discussion. Everyone should feel physically comfortable and be able to see all the other group members. While in discussion, try to speak to the whole group rather than directly to the tutor. Establish eye contact with everyone. If ideas always go back to the tutor for a response then discussion never really gets going. For a discussion *between students* to take off, eye contact and seating are important.

Clear goals

Make sure the goals of the discussion are clear. A meeting has an agenda, so ask the tutor what the topic/s and examples will be for the next week. Make sure you prepare. How can you discuss material you have not read? Read the primary text(s) concerned and as much secondary material as you have time for. Make notes on your reading and have important passages marked so you can locate them quickly in the seminar. The discussion needs to be focused and stay on topic to be useful.

Openness to new ideas

Try to go into the seminar with opinions as well as with an open mind. You need to have an open mind so you can hear other people's ideas, but the discussion needs to start with opinions. Don't be afraid of disagreement; conversation will be tedious if everyone always agrees with each other, but phrase your points in a non-confrontational manner. You can start with phrases such as, 'I see your point but . . .', 'What about . . . ?' or 'I like that idea, but . . .'.

Listening well

Hone your listening skills. Are you actually hearing others or are you too busy thinking about what you're going to say? A discussion will never take off if the participants are responding to their own thoughts rather than each other's comments. Make sure you have understood what other members of the group have said. Don't be afraid to ask for elaboration or repetition. Often this will help other students as well.

Clarity

Good discussion is about speaking clearly as well as listening attentively. Enunciate, don't mumble, and address the group openly. If you are not quite sure what it is you are trying to say, try writing down a few words on a piece of paper, or formulate your idea as a question. Questions are an important part of the seminar. Being able to ask relevant and pertinent questions is a crucial skill in any conversation, formal and informal.

A relaxed attitude

If you find speaking in groups very difficult, there are certain strategies you can use to overcome your anxiety:

- talk to others about your nervousness, as you'll probably find fellow students who feel the same way and this can help boost your confidence
- try to speak in the first meeting – the longer you stay silent, the harder it is to make your first contribution
- start off answering a question you feel sure of
- if there is small group work, you can start off speaking here and work up to speaking in the whole group
- when you speak, look at the group members – you will see that they are listening and they are interested in what you have to say.

Theodore Zeldin writes:

> I don't think you have to be talkative to converse, or even to have a quick mind. Pauses in conversation do no harm. One of the most memorable conversationalists in history, the French diplomat Talleyrand, who suffered from a lonely upbringing and a physical handicap, would often sit through a party without saying a word, but then suddenly come out with a sentence which people said was the sort they never forgot. What matters is whether you are willing to think for yourself, and to say what you think.

> (Zeldin 1999: 15)

ACTIVITY 6:

Interview either a tutor or a student from a different course about what they think are the strengths and weaknesses of the seminar forum as a learning environment and their own experience of seminars. Prepare a list of questions beforehand and write a short commentary on the interview from the notes you have taken.

ACTIVITY 7:

This task is a group activity and should be time-limited to fifteen minutes. Imagine that as a group you have been shipwrecked on a desert island. As a group you have to come up with *any* eight items which have survived with you on the island. Decide on eight and then prioritise them into a list numbered 1–8 with no. 1 as the most valuable and no. 8 as the least valuable. Appoint an observer to take notes on the discussion as it progresses.

When the time is up, discuss how you achieved the task using the notes of the observer as an *aide-mémoire*. Did you manage to accomplish the task? Was everyone heard? Did the discussion turn into argument? Did certain voices dominate? Who took which roles and did they change (for instance were you a questioner, summariser, maker of statements, leader, initiator)? What strengths and weaknesses did you have as a group? Write up a short report on your group's performance.

ACTIVITY 8:

Over the next week keep a diary of the seminars you have attended and details of your own participation in them as well as the dynamics of the group as a whole. What have you achieved as a seminar participant? What areas could be improved by you and by the group as a whole?

ACTIVITY 9:

Design a pamphlet about seminars for students who are about to enter university but who have had no experience of seminars at school. What do they need to know and how can the material be best presented? Use no more than 500 words and use images if you can.

Chairing seminars

When we converse informally with friends or family we regulate our own conversations. There is no one listening in and refereeing our discussion. In a more structured, public or formal discussion group a chairperson is necessary to keep the discussion focused and to ensure that goals are achieved. Chairing a discussion requires excellent listening and speaking skills. Whether you are Jeremy Paxman on *Newsnight* or chairing a meeting at work, you need to facilitate the discussion in certain ways. A balance of voices is necessary to ensure that all points of view are heard and that the topic is discussed in a full manner. When dealing with a panel of guests, Jeremy Paxman asks questions to bring new voices into the conversation. As a chairperson, you need to see that no one person dominates, making sure the discussion is open and inclusive, but not hijacked. This often means politely cutting a person off to leave time for other voices. You need to make sure the discussion stays on the topic, so that the agenda is covered. In the context of a meeting, confrontation or argument may need to be deflected, whereas on *Newsnight* the chair may actively seek to stir up controversy by challenging a speaker, or pitting one against the other. The chair also needs to listen attentively so s/he can sum up the arguments of each side, or the discussion thus far.

Finally, the function of the chairperson is to get the group to agree to a set of aims and objectives and to see that the group meets those objectives within the time allocated. The chairperson will also regularly try to sum up any agreements reached by the group and test them out to see if everyone agrees.

ACTIVITY 10:

In ten minutes have a group discussion about a controversial topic that you all find interesting (for example: should smoking be banned in all public places?). Divide the group into two, one group for and one against, and have each group seated in a line facing the other. Appoint two observers who will sit on one side of the room and take notes about the discussion. The aim is combat. Each side tries to win the argument through reason. Each side has five minutes preparation time before the debate begins.

In a second ten minutes have a group discussion about the pros and cons of euthanasia. This time do not divide into for and against, but instead appoint a chair, sit in a circle and discuss the issue together. The aim is to come to some kind of consensus through discussion. The chairperson should lay out the objectives of the discussion and should ensure that these objectives are met within the time. Again appoint two observers who will take notes about the discussion.

At the end take a further ten to fifteen minutes to hear what the observers noted and then discuss which method worked better: the antagonistic or the co-operative method. Did you arrive at a conclusion in either discussion? What was the role of the chair in the second session? Did s/he make the discussion more effective? What roles did particular participants take in the discussion? In which situations or contexts would the different types of discussion be preferable or useful?

Summary

In this chapter we have introduced you to:

- conversation in history
- methods and terminology for analysing conversation
- listening and asking questions
- gender and conversation
- seminar skills and techniques
- chairing skills.

References

Austen, J. (1985) *Emma* [1815]. London: Penguin.
Hurston, Zora Neale (1986) *Their Eyes Were Watching God*. London: Virago.

Pinter, H. (1991) 'The Applicant' in *Plays: Three*. London: Faber.

Shields, C. (1998) *Larry's Party*. London: Fourth Estate.

Tannen, Deborah (1992) *You Just Don't Understand: Women and Men in Conversation*. London: Virago.

Thoreau, Henry David (1999) *Walden* [1854]. Oxford: Oxford University Press.

Zeldin, T. (1998) *An Intimate History of Humanity*. London: Vintage.

Zeldin, T. (1999) *Conversation: How Talk can Change your Life*. London: Harvill.

Rhetoric and argument

Rebecca Stott

I n the last chapter we looked at the conventions of conversation, looking finally at the seminar as a formal version of the conversation, managed by a seminar leader and time-limited. When people gather for a seminar or a tutorial, they gather together not for social interaction but for *argument*. They meet to consider a book, or a body of ideas, not only to discuss it but to come to understand it better through argument. Their understanding of the subject will have changed by the end of the one-hour or two-hour period. That transformation will have come about through a democratic process, through a mutual exchange of ideas and questions.

In this chapter we will be looking at a crucial part of academic study – argument. It is crucial to both writing and speaking. We will be looking at how argument works, the conventions and structures of argument, and the skills needed for successful argumentation. Secondly we will be looking at rhetoric as the ancient art of persuasion, an art still used today in various forms to persuade people through argument.

Argument

What do we mean by argument and why is it such an important part of academic study? Argument is often seen as negative, a kind of breakdown of order and harmony, a sign that something is wrong between people ('they've been arguing a lot recently', we might say of two people and by that mean things are not good between them). Yet we also use the word argument to describe the formal reasoning in an essay, for instance. We say 'what are you arguing here?' or 'define your argument more clearly'. The ambiguity in the word here is instructive. The word argue comes from the original Latin word 'arguere', which means three things primarily: to make clear, to prove and to accuse. Perhaps when we talk about argument in the negative sense, as evidence of disharmony between two people, we are talking about a kind of arguing that is accusatory, concerned with victory not truth, and where the dialogue is full of abuses of power, unclarified prejudices and ambiguities. For the purposes of this book we define argument as *a communicative process used for the growth of knowledge, a process based upon making claims, asserting and challenging, assenting and dissenting*. It is conversational in form, involves critical reasoning, and depends upon participants coming to the argument prepared to reach an agreement.

Resolving conflict

Much social conflict is resolved through this kind of argument. Think of the Good Friday peace agreement made in Ireland in 1998. For months the press reported on the negotiations and persuasions that were going on behind closed doors to bring the key players in the conflict 'to the table'. Nothing could begin properly until those people agreed to be part of the negotiations, to actually 'come to the table'. The persuasions involved politicians and intellectuals from all over the world. Before peace negotiations could begin, conditions had to be met, conditions set by both sides: a cease-fire and a handing in of weapons. But the most important conditions expected of both sides were that those who came to the table came prepared to listen and to reach an agreement, even if that meant giving up on some of their own priorities or making serious compromises.

Think of the historical realities those people had to overcome to sit down and talk – decades of violence, past peace agreements and cease-fires that had broken down, and hundreds of deaths. Through the night they came together and made an agreement that aimed to bring about an end to violence in Northern Ireland. They achieved it through argument, through arguing over a document that had taken years to draw up and modify; they amended parts of it, discussed its implications and eventually signed up to it. No doubt there were raised voices, no doubt some people had to leave the room from time to time. There were periods in which every one felt they had reached a stalemate and no further progress was possible. Then someone will have asked a question in a slightly different way or made a new suggestion and the dialogue will have started up again.

Argument is a form of conflict but the kind of argument we are talking about here is one in which the participants are prepared to reach an agreement. The peace agreement of Northern Ireland depended in its final stages, then, on a number of articulate and well-informed people with stamina and open minds arguing around a table, and gradually moving towards an agreement. Many people who are trained for public life, for work as politicians, negotiators, and lawyers, are trained in argumentation because to be able to participate in decision-making in public life one must be able to argue in the most effective ways possible.

Argumentation goes on at every point in our lives, not only in the corridors and boardrooms of power. Think of the complex negotiations that go on in family life. Not all parents are prepared to reason with their children on all issues. There simply isn't the time in the day. It would be impossible to maintain a peaceful household if all rules were continually up for negotiation. However, many parents find that teenagers begin to question authority and to question the rules of the communities they live in (school or home) as they get older. Sometimes they will oppose authority through emotional or physical violence, or just plain disobedience. At best they will try to engage those in positions of authority over them in argument and will be prepared to reach agreements.

Analysing argument

What are the conventions and patterns of formal argumentation? There are several ways of analysing the conventions of argumentation but one of the simplest ways is to use the terms *claimant* and *interlocutor*. Imagine a teenager, Sarah, who wants to be allowed to go to an all-night party for the first time. She must try to persuade her parents and she will use a number of means to achieve this. She will appeal to their reason. First she has to make her claim – 'I should be allowed to go to Jane's party' – and she must choose a moment when her parents are most likely to listen. The conditions for the argument must be right. If they do listen she might support her claim by arguing that she is responsible, that she will be safe, and that people who her parents trust will be there. But she will only make these arguments if her parents agree to listen. They might for instance have said 'you're not going because I say so' and in this case Sarah's attempt at being a claimant has been denied by her parents who are in a position of power over her. It is only when they listen and engage with her claim that an argument takes place. When the argument begins, they might counter her claims by saying that there are still too many risks, that she has not yet proved herself responsible and so on.

In this scenario, Sarah is the claimant – she is bringing the claim 'to the table'. Her parents are the interlocutors – they are responding to her claim and refining it through questions, objecting to it, putting forward counter-claims, and producing their own evidence to support the new claims. Sarah may win or lose her claim, but as a group they are more likely to reach new positions through the process of arguing if all of them are prepared to reach an agreement. Conditions may be set on Sarah's attendance at the party, concessions may be made, or the old rules might remain in place and her parents' position on all-night parties will be remade through argument. It might also be possible that in the course of argument it becomes clear that actually Sarah's mother and Sarah's step-father have slightly different views on all-night parties and they haven't really addressed them before. In this case Sarah's mother might disagree with Sarah's step-father but still not wholly agree to Sarah's claim. Sarah's mother might herself become a claimant and Sarah might become an interlocutor to her mother's claim. The point we want to make here is that in the course of argument the participants will usually switch roles, moving effortlessly between being in the positions of claimant and interlocutor.

ACTIVITY 1:

Write a short account of an argument you have had with someone recently in which differing points of view have been resolved through argument. In what ways are the terms claimant and interlocutor useful for analysing the structure and progression of that argument?

ACTIVITY 2:

Even if we are arguing with ourselves, we change roles constantly between claimant, interlocutor and audience. Look at the following sketch of a thought-process. The thinker is trying to work out whether to apply for an MA programme after she has finished her degree. Read it through and identify the reasons the student explores for and against doing the MA. List them. Also try to identify roughly how many times the student changes role between claimant and interlocutor. The audience role is more difficult to identify in this kind of internal dialogue. The audience is the person or persons who are to be persuaded. Who is the assumed audience here? Who else might the student be trying to persuade apart from herself?

I want to do the course. I know that. And the course is interesting. I'd be studying all the writers who I'm really interested in and I'd be able to write a dissertation at the end of it on Woolf if I wanted to and I've never had the chance to work on her writing at length as an undergraduate. And I'm likely to get the grades I'll need in order to apply. But what would I be using it for? What would be the point of it? Do I just want to do it to postpone making a career decision for another year or do I want to do it for its own sake? Will it actually get me anywhere? If I'm going to be a teacher then an MA will help my career. People say that promotion comes more quickly if you've got an MA. But I don't know that I do want to be a teacher. And even if I do make up my mind that I want to be a teacher, I'm definitely not ready to do a PGCE yet. But I might be by next September. But that's another good reason isn't it? I mean doing an MA will give me more time to make up my mind about what I want to do next. But what about the money? Can I really justify the money which I'd have to borrow through a career development loan? Then I'd be stuck with the repayments on that for years and that would force me into a job more quickly in order to pay off the debts. Maybe I should apply for a grant then? But there's so much paperwork and I'll never be ready to get the forms in by March. But if I can't justify borrowing the money, I'll have to make myself apply for the grant. Maybe that's it then. I'll do the MA if I get the money from the grant-people. I'll put in an application before March and I'll wait and see. If I don't get it I'll get a job and apply to do the PGCE for the following year. That way I can use the intervening year to save up money to help fund the PGCE.

What are the key features of formal argument?

There will usually be:

- a claimant (who brings a claim)
- an interlocutor or interlocutors (who respond to the claim)
- an audience (who will or will not be persuaded by the argument)
- the participants will use reason to reach an agreement
- the premise on which the argument is based will be adapted to the particular audience.

What are the skills needed for effective argument?

The following qualities and skills are important components in the ability to argue effectively:

- openness to the positions of others
- good listening skills
- being able to reason effectively
- being able to ask good questions
- being able to collect appropriate evidence
- being able to see the sequence of an argument
- being able to summarise accurately the positions of others
- being able to think around an issue
- being able to speak so that people will listen
- clarity
- concision
- confidence
- good judgement.

Politicians, for instance, need to foster these skills. Argument, reason and dialogue are at the heart of a democratic society where people must be persuaded, not forced, to do things. Being able to persuade a population that the welfare state needs to be reformed in a number of key ways may win or lose an election. Good arguments will always take into account the needs and interests of the audience being addressed.

ACTIVITY 3:

Conduct an interview either by letter, e-mail or in person with someone in a public position who uses skills of argumentation on a regular basis (this might be someone you know or someone you know of – a police officer, a judge, lawyer, politician). Write out a list of questions beforehand based on some of the questions and issues raised in this chapter. The aim is to ask the interviewee to reflect on what role argument plays in his or her job.

Participating in argument

An argument doesn't exist in isolation, as a set of logical prepositions on a piece of paper. It needs to be delivered, engaged with and judged. Logicians might argue that a proposition is true if it is logical. In this book we are more interested in effectiveness than abstract logic. This book is interested in the interaction between claimant, interlocutor and audience. We are interested in how groups reach a consensus and how people persuade them that x or y is true or plausible or the right way forward. This means that we are claiming that the ultimate assessment of the value of a particular point of view rests with the audience who are being persuaded. Good arguments are effective because they persuade a particular audience in a particular time and place.

The following is a transcript of a discussion of a number of books, recorded for a Channel Four programme called *Booked* in December 1998. Reading a transcript is not the same as listening to a conversation, of course, because conversation is full of pauses and 'ums' and 'ers' and fragments of sentences. This particular transcript has been punctuated and phrased for ease of reading. If possible read the transcript aloud in order to bring it as close to an actual conversation as possible. The joint chairpeople are David Aaronovitch and Nigella Lawson (Nigella is a kind of deputy) and the guests are all writers: Andrea Ashworth, Alain de Botton and Salman Rushdie. The guests have been asked to choose and introduce their favourite book of the year for the group to discuss. Salman Rushdie has just introduced the first book, called *Underworld* by Don deLillo.

Salman Rushdie: I think *Underworld* is the novel of DeLillo's life. He's been working his way up to this novel through a number of wonderful books. I think it has a very good chance of surviving.

David Aaronovitch: Nigella, you lead a pretty busy life. Were you pleased that Salman had recommended an 827-page epic? (Laughter)

Nigella Lawson: Well, now you mention it, I have to say, Salman, I did think, do I need to read a book like this? And I also have to say that – this is an awful confession to make – I bought *Underworld* when it first came out and I took it home and I kept thinking I was going to read it. I knew I wanted to read it, but I didn't. But you know the minute I started I just felt immensely grateful, I was cross with myself for not having started it earlier, but I just thought that it was so wonderful. You talk about the scope, but I loved the mix between the intimate and the epic which I think is amazing. At the very beginning – the baseball scene – when I started reading it, it was like a panning shot in cinema and I thought, how interesting, he's taking on what film can do and really this is what you would have in a film. And then as you carry on you realise that what he's doing actually is much more than film can do and he's reminding us about why we need writing. I just thought it was amazing.

David Aaronovitch: Alain. Could this book have been written by anybody other than an American?

Alain de Botton: No. And I think that's why – looking at it from England – one can't help but feel a certain sort of envy for something that's possible there that in a way perhaps is not possible here. One feels that he really is taking on the twentieth century and America with it and it's that scope, that ambition, that I admired. And he really does pull it off. There are boring passages – there are certainly bits one can skip – but there are others that are wonderful. I almost saw it as a collection of short stories that interlink, that's the way that it's really assembled. But, very impressive.

David Aaronovitch: Andrea, for me, one of the things that I really liked about this is the fact that he is a writer who is so literate about politics and culture, but he's actually pretty damn good about relationships and little things too.

Andrea Ashworth: I think so. I really was very much impressed by the sweep that Nigella just mentioned between the epic and then this kind of zooming in which is very cinematic; zooming in to the fine details, this amazing sort of virtuoso veracity of the way that our minds tick. And that's married to physical details. I have a real, adore/admire relationship with DeLillo (laughs). Sometimes I just adore the stuff; his prose is just sublime I think. I'm a real floozy for fine writing. And sometimes I think the artifice is a bit, it gets in the way I think, the prose is conspicuously sumptuous, and I can see that people would have trouble with that.

David Aaronovitch: Salman, clearly you are also a floozy for fine writing...

Salman Rushdie: ... always ...

David Aaronovitch: . . . as Andrea was. Who's going to get this in their Christmas stocking from you?

Salman Rushdie: Well, you know, I'm very relieved that everybody liked it, so I suspect that it might go into a lot of Christmas stockings. It is, you know, in this day and age, quite a lot to ask of people, that they give this much time and attention to a book and you really want to be sure that what you are going to get back from it is worth it. I've been reading the Tom Wolfe novel recently which unfortunately I think is just not worth it. You read an enormous amount of pages and when you've finished, all that you can feel is that you've finished, whereas with this, it stays with you, really, for ever. It's a work of visionary realism. It is very realistic, it does talk about the cold war period through the experience of ordinary people in the most brilliant way, but it also gives you a vision of America and the twentieth century which really stays with you.

David Aaronovitch: *Underworld* by Don DeLillo is published by Picador and costs £18. . . . Now, here's what Alain's friends will be finding in their Christmas stockings. *Atlas of the European Novel* by Franco Moretti. Moretti is a quirky Italian academic and this is a book about how geography has shaped the European novel. It uses examples from all sorts of European writers – Austen, Dickens, Balzac, Dostoyevsky, Conan Doyle – to try to show that where things happen in novels is just as important and revealing as why they do. It's illustrated with a series of offbeat and rather surprising maps, which plot out anything from the journeys the characters make in *Our Mutual Friend* to the places where the murders happen in Sherlock Holmes. This is a hoot really, isn't it?

Alain de Botton: It is. It's one of those mad academic books where an academic gets into their head that they're going to analyse something and they do it in such detail that, as you say, it is kind of almost comic. And the premise is that we're going to look at all the maps of where the action takes place in some classic nineteenth-century novels, which throws up all sorts of rather interesting things. For instance, he does an analysis of Sherlock Holmes and where all the murders take place in Sherlock Holmes. Now if one looks at this, one discovers that all the murders take place in the West End. Now Sherlock Holmes was writing at a time when all sorts of real murders were taking place in the East End but Conan Doyle puts them all in the West and Moretti has a rather interesting analysis where he says what Conan Doyle is essentially doing is denying the real reasons why people get murdered which is because of poverty and social conditions and setting it all in the West End in this rather exclusive world. He gives us a map, for instance, which I can show you, of where all the murders are taking place in Conan Doyle's novels and also in real life (shows map). So that's quite interesting. There are other maps . . .

David Aaronovitch: He does a similar trick for villains, doesn't he?

Alain de Botton: Yes. He spots where all the villains come from. Now all the villains tend to come from France (laughter) – an amazing number, all of these, in Dickens, in Mary Shelley, every time you get a baddie, it's French. And so there is a wonderful charting of that. It enables us to look at novels through another perspective.

David Aaronovitch: Salman, what did you think of it?

Salman Rushdie: Well, you know, in Thomas Pynchon's novel *Gravity's Rainbow*, there's a character who becomes very important to the Secret Service during the war because it seems as if his sexual progress through London, which has been charted on maps in MI5 because it seems to prefigure exactly the places where the bombs will drop in a few days time. So every time he gets off with a girl, you know, they put a pin and three days later there's a V2 rocket landing on that point, so it becomes a useful predictive mechanism. And I thought this book was sort of in that area of looniness (laughter).

Nigella Lawson: What do you feel about your novels being charted in that way? Of course it would be amusing, but do you think it would give any literary insight?

Salman Rushdie: Not very much I think. Just this much: I do think that if you, as I have done and Dickens for instance does a lot, write a lot of books about the same place, the same city – Conan Doyle is another example – you do sometimes begin to think, well, I'm using the same neighbourhood all the time. Maybe I should go to another neighbourhood.

David Aaronovitch: I'd love to see a chart showing where your characters fall out of aeroplanes.

Salman Rushdie: That's very easy, Pevensey Bay (laughter).

David Aaronovitch: Andrea. One of the lessons Moretti claims to learn from this is, English Euro-scepticism and its roots in the novel, isn't it?

Andrea Ashworth: It's very easy to map the insularity of the English novel. You don't need maps to do that. I think this is less a literary cartography than a literary history. Geography obviously is crucial in many novels, but without history – without being located in history – it doesn't mean very much. And I'd like to know, why is Jane Austen read in Japan? Geography can only explain the power of a novel so far and I think that the borders that get crossed, the journeys that get made in novels, are more importantly those between characters and within a character.

David Aaronovitch: You deny him almost entirely. Nigella, what did you think?

Nigella Lawson: Well, you know, in theory I think this is wonderful but I do suffer from a sort of cartophobia and so I look at it and my eyes sort of glaze over . . .

Andrea Ashworth: (Nodding) you just jump over the maps . . .

Nigella Lawson: I have a slight allergy to maps . . .

Andrea Ashworth: Me too. And figures . . . (laughter)

Nigella Lawson: I felt that the ideas are interesting but I don't want reading reduced to graphs and maps . . .

David Aaronovitch: Do you think this is a boy/girl thing . . . (laughter)

Salman Rushdie: I think also that the maps are very small, you have to use a magnifying glass . . .

Andrea Ashworth: They should have been bigger and they would have been more beautiful . . .

Salman Rushdie: . . . but I do think he's right sometimes; I think the thing he says about Conan Doyle, for instance, is largely true. He does show that he is denying the reality of the age in order to create these elegant fictions. And I think when he shows you how centralised publishing is as an industry, how publishing happens in very few places, it does say something about why writers gravitate to those places. So there are times when he does show you things that are interesting.

David Aaronovitch: Alan, defend the use of maps in a book such as this.

Alain de Botton: Yes, well he makes a very interesting point that the maps are not simply diagrams illustrating a point, they are points themselves and I think the visual element of books is very often left out. This is a book made up of text and maps and I think the maps are great fun. I love looking at maps. Some of these maps I don't understand at all and some of the fun of this book is that – once one gets to something like this – I don't know what's going on here at all (holding up a diagram) but I think it's fascinating and I just like to look at it, it's like looking at a very technical diagram and I think how clever and mysterious . . .

David Aaronovitch: Will you be only giving it to blokes?

Alain de Botton: No, no, I will be trying to educate my many female friends who have no sense of direction . . . (laughter)

Andrea Ashworth: Oh, that's a help!

David Aaronovitch: *Atlas of the European Novel* is published by Verso, price £16.

(*Booked*, A Diverse Production for Channel Four, December 1998)

ACTIVITY 4:

Read through the transcript above very carefully and consider the following questions:

- Do the participants change roles between claimant and interlocutor?
- Identify the places in the conversation where people are making claims. What are the claims? Summarise each in one sentence.
- What sort of phrases and expressions do the participants add to their statements to avoid sounding too dogmatic and to keep the discussion open (e.g. 'I think' or 'perhaps').
- Who is the assumed audience? How can you tell?
- Identify some of the disagreements in the discussion.
- How is the discussion structured? How successful is it for this context?
- Analyse the role of the chairpeople. What kinds of questions do they ask and how successful are they as questions?
- Write up your answers as a short report of about 500 words.

ACTIVITY 5:

Choose a subject you feel strongly about. Write down your own view on the subject as clearly and concisely as you can. If you are undecided, try to define exactly why you find it difficult to make up your mind. What is it about your background and experience that has led to you holding this view? Now try to come up with three plausible imaginary characters who because of their own experience or background are likely to express views on the subject quite different from the one you have identified. Write down short notes on the three characters, their positions, and how they came to form these opinions.

Now script a five-minute debate, with a chair, for a radio programme on the subject aimed at a specific audience. Decide on the audience before you begin. Think about what evidence your chosen characters might use to defend their positions. You will need an introduction by the chairperson, who will set the context of the debate and draw the audience's interest as well as introducing your panel. The chair should ask good questions and keep what is likely to be a very heated discussion under some control. Make sure that as wide a range of views as possible is aired and that your participants move between the different roles of claimant and interlocutor.

Alternatively, if you are working in a group, you could improvise a debate on the subject, with members of the group role-playing the characters you have chosen. You should ensure that each of you represents a slightly different position on the subject from the others. Everyone should be sure of who they are, what they think and why they think it. You should appoint a chairperson whose role is to introduce the discussion and direct it, by asking questions and ensuring that everyone has a chance to express themselves. The chairperson should also ensure that the participants argue with each other and ask each other questions. Begin your ten-minute debate when everyone is ready and in character. Improvise. No rehearsal!

Rhetoric

So far we have looked at conversation and at argumentation as a formal kind of conversation. Where does rhetoric fit in and why is it important in thinking about argument and persuasion? Rhetoric means 'the arts of persuasion' and it is as old as the ancient Greeks. A rhetor was an ancient Greek or Roman teacher of rhetoric. When we say that a piece of writing is rhetorical we mean that it has been written with a view to persuasive effect. A rhetorical question is not a question that requires a direct answer but a question which has been used to create a particular effect. Throughout this chapter I have been using them. I have used one in the second sentence of this particular paragraph. In asking that question I didn't expect all my readers to answer the question; rather I used it to focus my paragraph and to present a question that I would then set out to answer. It created the right effect at the right time. I needed to show where I was heading and what was going on in my thinking processes at this point in my chapter. Rhetorical questions are only one of hundreds of rhetorical techniques identified by the ancient Greeks.

Rhetoric is the art of persuading people. It is a body of knowledge produced by philosophers and orators over thousands of years. It is not easy to explain in a short chapter. The first people to define rhetoric lived nearly 2,500 years ago. Aristotle, the great Greek philosopher who lived 300 years before Christ, wrote a book called *Rhetoric* in which he defined rhetoric as the art of 'discovering all the available means of persuasion in any given case'. This was one of the very first and simplest definitions. Aristotle insists that rhetoric can adapt to any new subject area. It is possible to find the means of persuasion for any given subject. His book outlines all the means and devices by which an orator can persuade an audience of his or her point of view. These devices are emotional as well as intellectual.

Aristotle classifies the means of persuasion into three main categories:

- *ethos*: persuasion through personality and stance
- *pathos*: persuasion through the arousal of emotion
- *logos*: persuasion through reasoning.

After Aristotle, one of the most famous Roman rhetoricians, Quintillian (writing in AD 94), analysed the text of a persuasive rhetorical text or speech as consisting of

- *invention*: the finding of arguments or proofs
- *disposition*: the arrangement of such matters
- *style*: the choice of words, verbal patterns and rhythms that will most effectively express the material.

Later rhetoricians came to refer to three main categories of oratory:

- *deliberative*: to persuade an audience to approve or disapprove of a particular point of view or policy (e.g. parliamentary address)
- *forensic*: to achieve condemnation or approval of a person's actions (e.g. in a court of law)
- *epideictic*: the use of rhetoric, usually in a ceremonial context, to enlarge on the praiseworthiness (or sometimes the blameworthiness) of a person or group of persons.

Rhetoric in history

Rhetoric grew with the emergence of democracies because within a democracy people have to be persuaded not ruled by force. The Greeks and Romans needed the arts of persuasion because they ran partially democratic political systems. I say partially because democracy means government by all the people, either directly or through representation; it is easy to forget the use of slavery in ancient Greece and Rome. Were you aware that these political systems were only democratic up to a point? Rhetoric was used in the law courts and in the political assemblies. As the power of the Greek and Roman empires declined, so did rhetoric, although it had an important place in the early years of the Christian church right up to the time of St Augustine.

After the collapse of the Roman Empire feudalism spread across Europe. This is a term used to describe a form of government which was very hierarchical, based upon landownership and the obligation of all those who worked on the land (vassals) to serve and pay homage to the lord who ruled through the feudal manor. It was a system of monopoly rights. Rhetoric held its own in the monasteries and their schools but disappeared elsewhere – there was no need to spend time persuading the people when you could simply rule them by force. But at the same time rhetoric moved into written forms in prologues to scholarly editions. It also passed into preaching, into drama and into satire. William Langland, for instance, wrote a satirical poem called *Piers Plowman* which used rhetorical devices to express political and religious discontent. From the early medieval period rhetoric was studied as one-third of the university curriculum, closely related to dialectic (logic) and grammar; this curriculum was called the Trivium because it was divided into these three parts. Do you think there is a place for the study of rhetoric in universities today?

So, how did rhetoric become popular again? During the Renaissance in Europe in the fourteen and fifteenth centuries the complete works of the rhetoricians Aristotle and Quintilian were rediscovered, reprinted and circulated. This could not happen until the spread of printing, of course. However, the use of rhetoric in politics was limited because throughout Europe political autocracy was still dominant. Because of the new availability of texts through printing, rhetoric had a huge influence on the rising art form, drama. Playwrights such as Marlowe (who is known to have attended grammar school) and Shakespeare (who is assumed to have gone to grammar school) were trained in rhetoric and often used it to subvert the political, religious and social order of the day. We will investigate Shakespeare's use of rhetoric in more detail in the next chapter of this book.

Rhetoric continued to be taught in schools up until the eighteenth century, but in the nineteenth century it was rarely taught as a separate subject. With the rise of the public schools, public speaking and debate forms were taught but not as a formal programme of rhetoric. Rhetoric, however, was an important part of the writing of the Victorians, who were very much concerned with argumentation and persuasion about a number of important social, philosophical, political, scientific and literary issues from the role of the government in poor relief to the enfranchisement of women. Rhetorical devices are embedded in much of what we would recognise as Victorian styles of writing in many different genres. It was very much an age of persuasion. Before moving on to consider the role of rhetoric today, you might like to look back over this brief history and trace the connections between rhetoric and democracy.

Where is rhetoric today?

Rhetoric, the art of persuasion, is all around us today. Its omnipresence has been particularly facilitated by the media explosions of the second half of the twentieth century. Persuasion is used for many purposes from formal speeches in the House of Commons to selling a car in a car showroom. If rhetoric is defined as the means of persuasion in any given case, then we can see how adaptable it is. It has had to be adaptable, because like language it has to adapt to the needs of each successive generation. There is a great deal of variation within political speeches for instance – politicians such as Tony Blair and Margaret Thatcher have different styles of oratory but they both use rhetorical devices. If we were to search for rhetoric in contemporary society we would find it in television interviews of a political nature, in discussion programmes, in academic books, in lectures, in the editorial columns of newspapers, in government statements, in charity fund-raising and in advertising.

Politicians need to be able to persuade people these days in so many different contexts and situations – on television, in the street, in debate, in the House of Commons. Their means of persuasion must adapt to the people to whom they are speaking. A speech delivered to a group of European business people in a large hotel is unlikely to work if it is delivered to a group of local Labour activists meeting in a pub. Although the basic premises of the argument may remain the same, the speech will need to be adapted for each audience. The means for persuasion in the two cases are unlikely to be the same.

Rhetorics

Many contemporary theorists of rhetoric talk about rhetorics rather than rhetoric. This is because they recognise that the conventions of argumentation differ in many different societies and cultures. There are different styles and protocols of reasoning around the world. It is important not to generalise about processes of reasoning, to assume that the rhetorical methods of academic essay writing we use in British universities will be the same in for instance Japanese universities and so on, or assume that the values and beliefs of one audience will be the same as another. Writers who are concerned to persuade must do so within the reasoning conventions of their particular culture and community. All persuasion must adapt to the needs and expectations of the audience.

The ethics of rhetoric

In a book by the Greek philosopher Plato called *Gorgias*, Socrates denounced rhetoric as a kind of box of tricks. He drew attention to the fact that good orators could sell people false ideas. People today sometimes use the term 'mere rhetoric' or 'empty rhetoric'; what they mean is that the speaker is using rhetorical tricks without integrity to persuade people. The argument does, of course, hold water. A car salesperson, for instance, might use any proven methods of persuasion to sell a car, regardless of his real opinion of the car. However, the fact that rhetoric can be used to sell false ideas is not a reason for rejecting it.

First of all, we believe that the study of rhetoric has a vital role to play because rhetoric is an important part of a democratic society – if you believe that agreement is important, you must be able to persuade people, not simply impose your will upon them. Therefore respect for the intelligence of your audience and integrity of purpose are at the heart of effective communication. Secondly, the study of rhetoric is important because as members of a democratic society we will be surrounded by people making claims upon us all the time. A working knowledge of rhetorical devices will help us to be more critical and discerning listeners and readers and therefore better citizens. Thirdly, as readers, a knowledge of rhetoric is central because all writers are in some ways making claims upon us and a working knowledge of rhetoric will help us see how they are trying to persuade us. It will help us to be better readers. Finally, as writers and interpreters of literature we need to be able to persuade our readers that our analysis of the text is accurate. Therefore rhetoric will help us to be better writers and critics.

Analysing rhetoric

What makes effective rhetoric? We can consider this by analysing the two formal speeches given below. The first is Tony Blair's first speech as Prime Minister, delivered to party workers and their families after his general election victory in May 1997. The second is an extract from Hilary Rodham Clinton's speech at the Fourth World Conference on Women in Beijing,

China, in 1995. As you read them through, consider the following list of questions:

- What is the speaker trying to say or argue? What is the speaker's claim?
- How is the argument structured? Identify the different parts of the argument.
- How does the speaker use emotional or logical means of persuasion?
- Word choice – what kinds of words are chosen?
- Register – is it appropriate to the audience?
- Does the speaker use any of the following features and to what effect?
  - sound patterning (alliteration, repetition, assonance, dissonance, etc.)
  - figurative language (metaphors, similes, imagery, personification, etc.)
  - antithesis (one idea pitted against its opposite)
  - puns and word-play
  - syntactic devices (parallel sentences, repeated clause structures within one sentence)
  - listings
  - repetition
  - amplification and diminution (playing up and playing down)
  - rhetorical questions
  - climaxes
  - irony.

Speech 1

I have just accepted Her Majesty the Queen's kind offer to form a new administration and government for the country. John Major's dignity and courage over the last few days and the manner of his leaving is the mark of the man. I am pleased to pay tribute to him.

As I stand here before 10 Downing Street I know all too well the huge responsibility that is upon me and the great trust that the British people have placed in me. I know well what this country has voted for today. It is a mandate for New Labour and I say to the people of this country – we ran for office as New Labour, we will govern as New Labour. This is not a mandate for dogma or for doctrine, or for a return to the past, but it is a mandate to get those things done in our country that desperately need doing for the future. And this new Labour government will govern in the interests of all our people – the whole of this nation. That I can promise you.

When I became leader of the Labour party some three years ago I set a series of objectives. By and large I believe we have achieved them. Today we have set objectives for new Labour Government – a world-class education system. Education is not the privilege of the few but the right of the many. A new Labour Government that remembers that it was a previous Labour Government that formed and fashioned the welfare state and the National Health Service. It was our proudest creation. It shall be our job and our duty now to modernise it for a modern world, and that we will also do.

We will work in partnership with business to create the dynamic economy, the competitive economy of the future. The one that can meet the challenges of an entirely new century and new age and it will be a government that seeks to restore trust in politics in this country. That cleans it up, that decentralises it, that gives people hope once again that politics is and always should be about the service of the public. And it shall be a government, too, that gives this country strength and confidence in leadership both at home and abroad, particularly in respect of Europe.

It shall be a government rooted in strong values, the values of justice and progress and community, the values that have guided me all my political life. But a government ready with the courage to embrace the new ideas necessary to make those values live again for today's world – a government of practical measures in pursuit of noble causes. That is our objective for the people of Britain.

Above all, we have secured a mandate to bring this nation together, to unite us – one Britain, one nation in which our ambition for ourselves is matched by our sense of compassion and decency and duty towards other people. Simple values, but the right ones.

For 18 years – for 18 long years – my party has been in opposition. It could only say, it could not do. Today we are charged with the deep responsibility of government. Today, enough of talking – it is time now to do.

(http://www.ukpol.co.uk/blair.shtml)

Speech 2

I believe that, on the eve of a new millennium, it is time to break our silence. It is time for us to say here in Beijing, and the world to hear, that it is no longer acceptable to discuss women's rights as separate from human rights. These abuses have continued because, for too long, the history of women has been a history of silence. Even today, there are those who are trying to silence our words.

The voices of this conference and of the women at Huairou must be heard loud and clear. It is a violation of *human* rights when babies are denied food, or drowned, or suffocated, or their spines broken, simply because they are girls. It is a violation of *human* rights when women and girls are sold into the slavery of prostitution. It is a violation of *human* rights when women are doused with gasoline, set on fire and burned to death because their marriage dowries are deemed too small. It is a violation of *human* rights when individual women are raped in their own communities and when thousands of women are subjected to rape as a tactic or prize of war. It is a violation of *human* rights when a leading cause of death world-wide among women ages 14 to 44 is the violence they are subjected to in their own homes. It is a violation of *human* rights when young girls are brutalised by the painful and degrading practice of genital mutilation. It is a violation of *human* rights when women are denied the right to plan their own families, and that includes being forced to have abortions or being sterilised against their will.

If there is one message that echoes forth from this conference, it is that human rights are women's rights . . . And women's rights are human rights.

(http://www.whitehouse.gov/WH/EOP/First_Lady/html/generalspeeches/1995/plenary.html)

ACTIVITY 6:

Compare the speeches by Tony Blair and Hilary Clinton and address the questions set out in the list above. What are the speakers trying to achieve and *how* do they do it? What are their claims? Try to identify as many different kinds of rhetorical devices as you can. What are the differences between the two speeches in terms of content and form? Why might these differences exist? Make notes and write up a summary report.

ACTIVITY 7:

In this book we have argued that all argument is dialogical. We mean by this that no argument can happen with only one person. Even if someone is having an argument with themselves inside their own head, then they are inventing different positions for themselves in order to have the debate. Therefore anybody who wants to lay out an argument to an audience must be aware of what an interlocutor would say and address that imaginary interlocutor in the speech. Even a monological speech (one person speaking in front of an audience) is implicitly dialogical.

Imagine you have been asked to be the interlocutor for Hilary Clinton's speech. How would you question or argue in response to it? What would the grounds be for opposition? Remember your opposition needs to be based on reason not unexamined prejudices.

ACTIVITY 8:

Write a two-minute speech (less than one sheet of A4) arguing for something you feel strongly about. Use any of the rhetorical devices that you think work well in either of these speeches by Tony Blair or Hillary Clinton. You are addressing a political rally with a large crowd so you will need to move as well as inform your crowd.

Identify the audience you will be addressing before you begin. Can you be sure you are addressing all the different kinds of people who will be in the crowd? What questions might they want to ask of you if they were able to? Next think about the positions an interlocutor might take so that you can take these positions into account in your speech.

Once you have thought through these questions, begin to structure your speech. You will need to begin by deciding *what* you want to say and then *how* you are going to say it. Follow the famous rhetorical stages: *invention*: the finding of arguments or proofs; *disposition*: the arrangement of such matters; *style*: the choice of words, verbal patterns and rhythms that will most effectively express the material.

ACTIVITY 9:

Find someone who holds views on a subject which are very different from your own (this might be a fellow student or a neighbour or relative, for instance). Interview them about their views on this subject. You aim is simply to understand their view as fully as possible, not to intervene or contradict. Write up a short report which summarises their view fairly and fully without judgement or comment. Then write a short report on your view presented fairly and fully without judgement or comment. Now test the objectivity of your account by giving it to a third person (not someone who knows you well) to see if they can tell which position is yours from the language alone. Is bias detectable in your account?

Summary

In this chapter we have introduced you to:

- argument and the resolution of conflict
- methods for analysing argumentation
- argumentation skills and their place in the world
- rhetoric in history
- the ethics of rhetoric
- speech-making
- methods for analysing speeches.

CHAPTER 3

Shakespeare and Renaissance rhetoric

Nigel Wheale

I n the previous chapter we looked at the history of rhetorical argument and we examined the ways in which similar skills have been used in contemporary TV debates and political addresses. In this chapter we will consider the place of rhetoric in the work of one of the world's most successful speech-writers – William Shakespeare. In 1999 Shakespeare was voted the UK's choice as 'Personality of the Millennium', and there are over 300 film adaptations of his plays, more than for any other author. Shakespeare's drama has exercised a unique influence on writers for over three centuries and continues to occupy a central position in literary studies. Now we shall look more closely at the importance of rhetoric in Shakespeare's own day, and the ways in which rhetorical games contribute to the powerful magic which his dramas create in the theatre, on the film or TV screen, and when we act or read them ourselves.

Politics, class and rhetoric in Shakespearean England

By the late sixteenth century, and for the first time in European history, significant numbers of ordinary people were learning to read and write. These skills were still largely restricted to men from the middling ranks of society who lived in the larger towns, though increasingly women were also beginning to acquire some literacy. But women were not yet admitted to the grammar schools which taught Latin and Greek, nor would they be allowed to attend universities until the nineteenth century. Rhetoric, the ability to exercise eloquent power, was the Renaissance equivalent of our 'information technology revolution'. An important consequence was that the precious (and expensive) skills of literacy and eloquence could be fiercely resented by those who did not possess them.

In the turbulent fourth act of Shakespeare's *Henry VI (Part Two)*, one of his earliest plays, the Kentish revolutionary Jack Cade menaces London and threatens all established hierarchy. Shakespeare's Cade enters the stage accompanied by Dick the butcher, Smith the weaver, a sawyer and a crowd representing 'infinite numbers' of followers. Addressing these 'good people', Cade offers a radical reform programme and articulates grievances that were widespread in the 1590s, a decade troubled by bad harvests, urban insurrection and food riots. Suddenly, Cade's associates drag a schoolmaster in front of him: his crime is that he 'can write and read, and cast accompt' (is numerate). Cade pretends to be appalled by the clerk's 'elitist' skills (though in fact he knows that he routinely makes use of them himself). The schoolmaster had been found setting writing exercises for his boy pupils, and he carries 'a book in his pocket with red letters in't' – Cade's cronies decide that therefore he must be a witch! In order to capitalise on his followers' grievances, Cade puts the teacher on trial, simply because of his learning:

> **Cade:** Come hither, sirrah, I must examine thee . . . Dost thou use to write thy name? Or hast thou a mark to thyself, like an honest plain-dealing man?
> **Clerk:** Sir, I thank God, I have been so well brought up that I can write my name.
> **All:** He hath confessed: away with him! He's a villain and a traitor.
> **Cade:** Away with him I say! Hang him with his pen and inkhorn about his neck.
>
> (*Henry VI (Part Two)* 4.2.79–90; Shakespeare 1991: 176)

This demonstration of calculated bigotry is depressingly familiar to us from so many examples in recent history: Stalin's purge of the intellectuals, scholars forced to carry typewriters slung around their necks in the Maoist 'Cultural' Revolution, Cambodia's Khmer Rouge killing anyone who happened to wear glasses at Year Zero, the beginning of a new 'cleansed' era. Cade exploits the resentment of the kind of men who feel they are made vulnerable by their own ignorance and he easily turns this suspicion of learning into violent hatred. Cade seizes London and orders the destruction of every significant building – the Tower, the Inns of Court, London Bridge, and the burning of 'all the records of the realm'. In every twentieth-century uprising, the television and radio stations are strategic locations which have to be controlled, and if the BBC had existed in fifteenth-century London Cade would certainly have invaded the studios.

For Cade the attack on feudal privilege, legitimised by the play's emphasis on popular grievances, is also an attack on the means of knowledge itself. A key moment in Cade's fundamentalist revolution is his trial of the Lord Chancellor precisely because he had promoted education in the country:

Thou hast most traitorously corrupted the youth of the realm in erecting a grammar school: and whereas, before, our forefathers had no other books but the score and the tally, thou hast caused printing to be used . . . It will be proved to thy face that thou has men about thee that usually talk of a noun and a verb, and such abominable words as no Christian ear can endure to hear. Thou hast appointed justices of peace, to call poor men before them about matters they were not able to answer. Moreover, thou hast put them in prison; and, because they could not read, thou hast hanged them; when indeed, only for that cause, they have been most worthy to live.

(4.7.29–37; Shakespeare 1991: 185–6)

Cade's speech is simultaneously absurd and terrifying, a delirious crescendo which assaults the material bases of all knowledge – schools, paper, print, and the structure of language itself, through the attack on grammatical knowledge.

Can we imagine the relevance of this strange, obsessive material for the average Elizabethan playgoer? There is almost certainly some joking which is directed against playwrights and the intellectual free-booters among the contemporary audience, a rather bitter kind of humour which mocks the means of its own advancement – the grammar schools and universities were already producing 'superfluous men' educated 'above' themselves and their station. And it may also be the case that Cade's attack on the fundamental bases of learning and the persuasive effect of rhetoric produced by the privileged elite actually strengthened the London audience's growing awareness that literacy was now unavoidable in their daily lives, a potential for each individual and for every act of administration. Two-thirds of the population still could not read or write in 1590, and for another century this might not be a serious disadvantage, but the future certainly lay in talk of nouns and verbs (see Wheale 1999).

Rhetoric from the earliest period to the Renaissance, therefore, did not mean simply 'ornamental speaking', but 'cogent and persuasive argument', and, as discussed in the previous chapter, from the beginning of its history there was a continuous, never-resolved debate as to whether 'rhetoric' was a spurious technique for seducing listeners (or readers) through the use of emotive devices, or whether it was a logical and philosophically respectable method for the exploration of serious argument. When the influence of rhetoric began to be seriously questioned in the late sixteenth century with the development of new kinds of logical deduction and more empirically based knowledge, bored students altered the name of their curriculum and coined a new term for tedious and irrelevant studies – they called them not the 'trivium' (the official title of the three-part medieval degree), but *trivial*. Shakespeare, as so often, was at the front of the crowd, and is the first recorded user of this new word, again in *Henry VI (Part Two)* when the Earl of Suffolk says 'We have but trivial argument' (3.1.241).

Rhetoric in the grammar schools

Rhetorical training was therefore absolutely central to the education which Shakespeare received at Stratford Grammar School during the 1570s. He would have studied rhetoric through imitation of examples, many of them from Latin authors. Renaissance education was consciously constructed to produce obedient, productive and God-fearing citizens, and rhetoric was central to this education in 'civic values' and religious belief. This essentially political function of rhetoric had also informed classical ideals of writing and speech-making. Cicero (106–43 BC), a politician and author at the centre of power in the late Roman Republic, was such an accomplished 'rhetor' that his speeches and letters quickly became models of good practice. He wrote: 'Wisdom without eloquence does too little for the good of states, but eloquence without wisdom is usually highly disadvantageous and never helpful . . . the man who equips himself with the weapon of eloquence, not to be able to attack the good of his country but to defend it, will be a citizen most helpful and most devoted both to his own interests and to those of his community' (Cicero 1949: 3–5).

Therefore Renaissance statesmen, politicians and writers thought of the practice of rhetoric as combining practical advantages with beautiful effects, teaching personal morality together with political beliefs. The male writers who were taught rhetoric during the educational expansion of the 1570s obviously appropriated these skills for their poems and plays and defended their compositions with the kinds of argument made by Cicero. Ben Jonson, one of the most successful poet-dramatists of the period, made exactly this kind of claim in 1620 in a book called *Timber, or Discoveries*:

> The Poet is the nearest borderer upon the orator, and expresseth all his virtues, though he be tied more to numbers [rhyme and rhythm]; is his equal in ornament, and above him in his strengths . . . because in moving the minds of men and stirring of affections – in which oratory shows and especially approves her eminence – he [the poet] chiefly excels.
>
> (Jonson 1995: 587)

The poets and playwrights of the Elizabethan Renaissance who were active during the 1590s had received their education during the 1570s when there was a significant expansion in the number of schools in England and a lot of new thinking about teaching and the nature of the curriculum. At this period only boys continued formal schooling beyond the age of ten and the only women to be taught were the daughters of the middle and upper ranks of society who received private tuition at home, with emphasis on domestic skills and 'decorative' social arts. At this time, then, rhetoric was effectively a male discipline, used for winning arguments in the 'public sphere' of politics, theology or literature, and very useful for gaining the patronage of a rich or influential person. There might be a significant, long-range continuity here in the gendered nature of conversation, discussed above in Chapter 1. Deborah Tannen's (1992) observation that male conversation can be characterised as 'report-talk' while women's conversation tends more to 'rapport-talk' may be compared to the ways in which boys and girls were encouraged to organise their speech during the Renaissance.

Conventional wisdom in the Elizabethan period dictated that women should behave in a modest and retiring fashion and restrict themselves to the 'private sphere' of domesticity, piety and motherhood. In fact gender relations and codes for gendered behaviour were never as simple as this: the monarch after all was an extraordinarily powerful woman who was perfectly able to conduct all affairs of state. This was also the period when more women were beginning to read and write; there were over 200 published female authors between 1600 and 1660, all keen to acquire the rhetorical tricks of their male contemporaries. But when they did break into print, these first women writers almost invariably felt it necessary to make an apology about daring to adopt a public voice, and modestly defended their work by claiming that they lacked the necessary education and training in rhetorical performance. We can now explore some of the tensions that existed between gender and the persuasive charms of rhetoric in a famous exchange between Juliet and Romeo.

Dialogue, gender, and a rhetorical duel

Successful argument, like successful drama, is always an active dialogue. Even when a character like Hamlet is alone on stage, talking in a soliloquy ('solus loqui' – I speak alone), he is still arguing through different positions and taking different views about his situation, in dialogue with himself. And of course the audience must be included within that single conversation, in that they are conversing in their thoughts with the character. This central exchange of conversation which must always occur between a text and its reader, or the play and its audience, was described as *dialogism* by the influential Russian critic Mikhail Bakhtin (see Pope 1998: 224).

There are always at least three active dialogues under way in a rewarding theatrical experience: the dialogue that characters hold within themselves, the dialogue between the stage and the audience, and of course the exchange of dialogue between roles on stage. One of the most formalised exchanges of dialogue between characters was developed in the classical Greek theatre where an argument was conducted head-on in alternating lines: this was called 'stitch rhyme' (stichomythia) because the alternating lines were so closely related. Shakespeare also tied together the lines of dialogue in exchanges between characters by using stitch rhyme, but in the first conversation between Juliet and Romeo there is another, more complicated kind of dialogue at work. At the end of Act 1, Romeo 'gate-crashes' the Capulet ball, sees Juliet across the crowded room, and immediately falls in love with her. Simultaneously the tragic action begins to unfold because he is recognised as an intruder by Tybalt, who denounces him to Juliet's father. The first conversation between the lovers is therefore already tense, already shadowed:

Romeo:
If I profane with my unworthiest hand
This holy shrine, the gentle sin is this,
My lips, two blushing pilgrims, ready stand
To smooth that rough touch with a tender kiss.
Juliet:
Good pilgrim, you do wrong your hand too much, (5)
Which mannerly devotion shows in this,
For saints have hands that pilgrims' hands do touch,
And palm to palm is holy palmers' kiss.
Romeo:
Have not saints lips, and holy palmers too? (9)
Juliet:
Ay, pilgrim, lips that they must use in prayer.
Romeo:
O then, dear saint, let lips do what hands do:
They pray, grant thou, lest faith turn to despair. (12)
Juliet:
Saints do not move, though grant for prayer's sake.
Romeo:
Then move not while my prayer's effect I take.
Thus from my lips, by thine, my sin is purged. (15)
[Kissing her.]
Juliet:
Then have my lips the sin that they have took.
Romeo:
Sin from my lips? O trespass sweetly urged!
Give me my sin again.
[Kissing her again.]
Juliet:
You kiss by th'book. (18)
Nurse:
Madam, your mother craves a word with you.

(*Romeo and Juliet*, 1.5.92–110; Shakespeare 1984: 85–6)

ACTIVITY 1:

If you are working in groups you could explore this dialogue by performing it in pairs. If you are working alone take a few moments to read through the exchange, preferably aloud, to have a sense of it in performance and off the page. Each character's statement is a rhetorical move in the game of courtship. Briefly and accurately summarise the argument after each character speaks; you could use a 'chorus' figure to do this.

Transpose the speech into modern English prose, keeping the tight rhetorical structure. Compare your transposition to the original. What has been lost or gained? Write up your findings as a short report of about 300 words.

ACTIVITY 2:

How can you relate Juliet's speeches here to their Renaissance cultural context and the period's conventional expectations for female piety, modesty and virtue? How does Juliet negotiate her position within these expectations? (Remember Juliet would have been played by a youth in all performances up to about 1662: does this alter the gender issues?) Given the Renaissance attitudes towards female education described above, do you think that Juliet is praising or mocking Romeo when she tells him 'You kiss by the book'? Write up your answers into a short report.

One final observation about the rhetoric in this passage: the lovers actually enact a sonnet through this conversation, Romeo speaking the first quatrain, and Juliet replying with the second quatrain. Romeo raises the stakes in line 9 by introducing a new question, just at the point where conventional sonnets also make a change of direction. The lovers share the third quatrain (Romeo consistently taking the initiative), and they also share the concluding rhyming couplet on 'sake/take'. Their rhetorical courtship in the sonnet then becomes actual as they kiss, moving beyond the sonnet, but still in a quatrain structure, 'purged/took/urged/book' – and the hard world of family politics interrupts them with the Nurse's urgent demand.

Rhetoric and the drama of persuasion

Shakespeare's career, beginning in the late 1580s and probably drawing to a close around 1612, coincided with the creation of the London theatre as a mass commercial urban entertainment. About 40,000 people each week crossed the Thames and paid between one penny and sixpence to watch plays on Bankside. One theatre historian has calculated that there were 15 million theatre visits made between 1590 and 1642 when the theatres were finally closed at the onset of the civil wars. This suppression of the theatres by Puritan-dominated Parliament was in one sense a testament to the state's fear of drama's rhetorical potential, and the Elizabethan playhouses had been located outside the City walls because the civic authorities actually disapproved of them as rowdy, godless, immoral and diseased places. But it is vital to remember that the plays were also put on simultaneously in the Court, where they were very popular, even though many people of the 'middling' sort disapproved of the drama.

The rhetorical resonance of plays dealing with the nature of political authority was increased by this requirement to speak to at least two quite distinct audiences on the Bankside and at the Court, together with a lively awareness that they also drew serious hostility from other sections of their society. It may be that the monarch and the Court appreciated the rhetoric of Elizabethan and Jacobean drama precisely because early modern politics relied so much on the theatrical staging of power through display and speech-making. In the age before mass communications, theatre and rhetoric were used to display and assert the legitimacy of the monarch to the political elite at Court and to the masses beyond them. Queen Elizabeth literally 'made a spectacle of herself' by touring the country and staying in great houses (she was also very canny, and thereby saved a lot of Court expenses).

One reason why the theatre and actors were regarded as being dangerous and subversive in this period was because they mimicked the most powerful political establishment so effectively. Actors were distrusted because they could change their status and personality through 'personation' (a significant new word in the decade of the 1590s), and perhaps most scandalous of all, of course, the boy actors changed their gender to take on the female roles – no women acted on the English public stage before 1660. This was another example of the way in which rhetoric belonged to the male sphere.

Television, video and cinema are our own contemporary mass urban entertainment, and there is little doubt that the Elizabethan and Jacobean dramatists would be working in the media industry if they were time-shifted to the present day. Shakespeare was probably commissioned to write two play scripts each year for his particular acting company, which was, needless to say, the most successful in the period. Just imagine having to turn out *Julius Caesar* closely followed by *Hamlet* within twelve months: perhaps our essay deadlines aren't so challenging after all! Writing persuasive rhetoric for the stage could pay good dividends; by 1597 Shakespeare had earned enough to be able to buy New Place, the biggest house on the market, back home in Stratford.

While our media today are overwhelmingly visual, in 1590 people tended to say 'Let's go *hear* a play', which suggests that Elizabethan and Jacobean playgoers concentrated on the rhetoric of the drama to a much greater extent than we rely on the movie script as the main focus of our attention: the

Hollywood definition of a writer as 'a schmuck with a word processor' is quite revealing in the way that it disparages the contribution made by mere language. In the Elizo-Jacobean theatre there was often no scenery, only a few props and even fewer 'sfx' (special effects); the costumes could be very splendid, cast-offs from elite patrons, but the main work in the early modern theatre was done by listening closely to the language. Most of Shakespeare's plays were staged in the open air between 2 p.m. and 4 p.m., with up to 2,000 people crammed into the playhouse, so all the locations, night scenes and battles had to be painted in words. Word-painting, or *ekphrasis* (see the definition in the next section), was one of the most important rhetorical strategies used by writers from classical times.

Rhetorical training was a powerful resource for everyone in the Renaissance theatre, from the playwrights to the actors, and including the audience. Educated playgoers took pleasure in following the argumentative construction of speeches and in the use of rhetorical figures. Rhetoric was also an aid to memory, since the actor could visualise the order of his speech like a building through which he was walking, and so could remember the material more easily. The adverts in newspapers today which promise to help you improve your memory actually use these same ancient techniques.

For these reasons Renaissance audiences were probably more acute listeners than we are: it's hard to imagine, but a very popular entertainment at the time was taking notes from sermons in church, and then going over the content back at home. The most learned preachers such as John Donne (who was an avid playgoer in his youth) used extremely elaborate rhetoric in their sermons and delivered them direct to their audience, without notes. A successful sermon delivery was therefore very like the performance of a dramatic soliloquy; the use of rhetoric brought together the church and the theatre, two Renaissance institutions which were usually radically opposed to each other.

We can now be more analytical about the ways in which Renaissance argument was structured, often very elaborately, through the use of question-and-answer forms and figurative language. We shall do this in order to appreciate how the highly emotive effects of Shakespeare's dramatic language are actually often achieved by a foundation of careful rhetorical structure.

Tropes: the building blocks of rhetoric

Here are twenty of the commonest rhetorical figures – you may be surprised to find how often you have been using classical rhetoric without realising it! This demonstrates the point that rhetoric and oratory didn't cease to exist when they fell out of favour at the end of the eighteenth century. Rather, readers, writers and speakers became less conscious of the all-pervasive presence of rhetorical structures and less calculating in their use. These figures are sometimes called 'tropes', meaning 'turns' in language which catch the attention of the reader or listener. The Greek words are marked to show where the stress occurs in pronunciation.

- *Alliteration*: repetition of the same consonant at the beginning of a sequence of words.
- *Anáphora*: repetition of the same word in succeeding clauses or sentences: 'If you did know to whom I gave the ring, / If you did know for whom I gave the ring, / And would conceive for what I gave the ring . . .' (continued for two more lines by Bassanio and then returned by Portia over four lines: *Merchant of Venice* 5.1.193–202).
- *Antithesis*: contrasting words and therefore ideas are placed close to each other: 'Among the faith*less*, faith*ful* only he' (*Paradise Lost* 5.897).
- *Aposiopésis*: 'the figure of silence or of interruption' (Puttenham 1968: 139): breaking off a sentence before completion, often indicating passionate feeling of one kind or another.
- *Assonance*: grouping of the same or similar vowels closely in a sequence of words: 'Why, I in this weak piping time of peace / Have no delight to pass away the time' (*Richard III* 1.1.24).
- *Climax*: Greek for 'ladder', repeating the final word in the first phrase or clause at the beginning of the second, the last of the second at the beginning of the third: 'Why, the whole world were but as an empire, that empire as a province, that province as a bank, that bank as a private purse . . .' (Jonson, *Volpone* 2.2.210).
- *Ekphrasis*: 'Ekphrasis is an account with detail; it is visible, so to speak, and brings before the eyes that which is to be shown. Ekphrases are of people, actions, times, places, seasons, and many other things . . . The special virtues of ekphrasis are clarity and visibility; the style must contrive to bring about seeing through hearing. However, it is equally important that expression should fit the subject: if the subject is florid, let the style be florid too, and if the subject is dry, let the style be the same' (Hermogenes of Tarsus, second century AD, in Baxandall 1971: 75). So, an ekphrasis was a vivid description, written in a style which attempted to match its subject. Ekphrasis was hugely influential in Renaissance art: painters such as Bellini, Michelangelo and Raphael were inspired by the ekphrases of Ovid and other classical poets, reproducing their allegories on canvas. Shakespeare would certainly have studied ekphrasis: an example in the plays might be Gertrude's detailed word-picture of Ophelia's drowning in *Hamlet* 4.7.165ff.
- *Erótema*: (not what it sounds like!) a rhetorical question, that is a question not expecting a reply but asked for the sake of emotional or logical emphasis: 'What is a man, / If his chief good and market of his time / Be but to sleep and feed?' (*Hamlet* 4.4.33–5).

- *Hypérbaton*: particular deviation from the expected word order: 'My soul shall thine keep company to heaven' (*Henry V* 4.6.16).
- *Hypérbole*: exaggeration to increase an effect: 'I loved Ophelia. Forty thousand brothers / Could not with all their quantity of love / Make up my sum' (*Hamlet* 5.1.266–8).
- *Irony*: usually *Antíphrasis*, using a word or statement in the opposite sense to what would normally be understood: 'A little water clears us of this deed' (Lady Macbeth in *Macbeth*, 2.2.65).
- *Metaphor*: describing one thing directly in terms of another which shares some characteristics with it, as when Hamlet talks of outwitting Claudius and his minions: 'I will delve one yard below their mines / And blow them at the moon' (*Hamlet* 3.4.209–10). Metaphor is therefore an *implicit* comparison, while simile is an *explicit* comparison using a comparative (see below).
- *Onomatopoeia*: the trope where the sound of words mimics or reinforces their meaning: 'Blow, winds, and crack your cheeks! Rage, blow, / You cataracts and hurricanoes' (*King Lear* 3.1.1).
- *Oxymóron*: a phrase using contradictory terms to heighten meaning: 'Parting is such *sweet sorrow*' (*Romeo and Juliet* 2.1.229).
- *Párison*: repetition of a particular grammatical construction in linked clauses or sentences: 'Who is here so base that would be a bondman? If any, speak, for him have I offended. Who is here so rude that would not be a Roman? If any, speak, for him have I offended' (*Julius Caesar* 3.2.24).
- *Períphrasis*: an expansive way of describing something that might be said more concisely: 'Was this the face that launched a thousand ships / And burnt the topless towers of Ilium?' (that is to say, Helen of Troy: *Doctor Faustus* 5.1.97).
- *Prosopopóiea* or *Personification*: attributing human qualities to inanimate objects: 'Comets . . . Brandish your crystal tresses in the sky' (*Henry VI (Part One)* 1.1.2).
- *Puns*: in *antanáclasis* a word is repeated with two different meanings: 'Old Gaunt indeed, and gaunt in being old' (*Richard II* 2.1.74); in *paronomásia* there is a play on words which sound identical (homophones) but which have different meanings: *Falstaff*: '. . . hang me up by the heels for a rabbit sucker, or a poulter's *hare*', *Hal*: Well, *here* I am set' (*Henry IV (Part One)* 2.5.439).
- *Simile* or *Homoeósis*: likening one thing to another using a comparative, usually 'like' or 'as', traditionally regarded as weaker than metaphor, though for no good reason: 'It seems she hangs upon the cheek of night / As a rich jewel in an Ethiop's ear' (*Romeo and Juliet* 1.5.44–5).
- *Synécdoche*: similar to *metonomy*, replacing the whole or the general with a part (the crown for the monarch), or vice versa: 'So foul a sky clears not without a storm: / Pour down thy weather' (*King John* 4.2.108).

ACTIVITY 3:

Write your own definitions in modern English of each of these rhetorical tropes, giving an example.

Using tropes: *Julius Caesar*

In Act 3 of *Julius Caesar*, Brutus, the idealistic republican, faces a crowd of the plebeians in the Forum and has to justify the murder of Caesar which he organised with Cassius. The plebeians are dangerous because they are portrayed as being numerous, easily swayed and vengeful; they have to be manipulated by the small patrician elite of Rome to gain their political allegiance. Caesar was at the height of his popularity with the Roman populus, so Brutus is in a very difficult, indeed dangerous position. The crowd is screaming 'We will be satisfied! Let us be satisfied!' – Brutus might well be torn apart. How does he employ rhetoric to save his life and justify the apparently indefensible murder of the head of state?

> **Brutus:** Be patient till the last. Romans, countrymen, and lovers, hear me for my cause, and be silent that you may hear. Believe me for mine honour, and have respect to mine honour, that you may believe. Censure me in your wisdom, and awake your senses, that you may the better judge. If there be any in this assembly, any dear friend of Caesar's, to him I say that Brutus' love to Caesar was no less than his. If then that friend demand why Brutus rose against Caesar, this is my answer: not that I loved Caesar less, but that I loved Rome more. Had you rather Caesar were living, and die all slaves, than that Caesar were dead, to live all free men? As Caesar loved me, I weep for him. As he was fortunate, I rejoice at it. As he was valiant, I honour him. But as he was ambitious, I slew him. There is tears for his love, joy for his fortune, honour for his valour, and death for his ambition. Who is here so base that would be a bondman? If any, speak, for him have I offended. Who is here so rude that would not be a Roman? If any, speak, for him have I offended. Who is here so vile that will not love his country? If any, speak, for him have I offended. I pause for a reply.

> (*Julius Caesar* 3.2; Shakespeare 1986: 690)

ACTIVITY 4:

Read through Brutus's speech and consider the questions below. When you identify rhetorical features you must, of course, always think about why they have been used and what effect they create. Write up your notes into a short analysis of the speech.

- Does Brutus use ethos, pathos, or logos as means of persuasion? (See 'Defining rhetoric', Chapter 2).
- How many rhetorical figures can you identify in the passage?
- How effective are the tropes for this particular audience?
- Why does Brutus speak in prose, and not verse (as was customary of the ruling or upper classes in Shakespeare's plays)?

The first point to notice is that the speech is given in prose, not blank verse. This is an important distinction throughout Shakespeare's plays: Brutus probably speaks prose to the plebeians in *Julius Caesar* because he is presenting himself as a plain-spoken man of truth, avoiding what might have been seen as the more sophisticated and therefore socially exclusive register of poetry. Brutus assumes a no-nonsense, plain-speaking attitude when he addresses the commoners in prose. This is almost an anti-rhetorical device; he is hoping that his sincerity and integrity will 'speak for themselves'. Mark Antony, who speaks after Brutus, speaks in blank verse, and in so doing treats the plebeians as his social equal. Antony – or rather his strategic use of rhetoric – wins the argument.

Although Brutus's use of prose is intended to present him as a plain-spoken man of truth, his carefully constructed speech is packed with rhetorical devices designed to manipulate the emotions of his audience and to carry the day. He does not address his audience plainly as 'Citizens' but rather he calls them 'Romans, countrymen, and lovers'. This is called *periphrasis*, an expansive way of saying something – he might just have said 'Citizens'. Antony, on the other hand, addresses the audience with the famous words 'Friends, Romans, countrymen' – Antony is immediately more intimate, more winning, because he uses the less formal register of 'Friends', where Brutus begins with the civic, neutral 'Romans'. Antony uses more *pathos*, where Brutus uses *ethos*. In other words, Antony succeeds by appealing to the emotions (pathos) of his audience whereas Brutus appeals to their sense of morality (ethos).

Repetition and variation are important rhetorical strategies which ensure that your message is getting across without boring your listeners. Brutus uses a number of different forms of repetition for precisely this reason. He employs *párison*, repetition of the same grammatical construction, in a number of different sentences – 'hear me . . . Believe me . . . Censure me', and again in lines 9 to 11 in a climactic series, 'weep . . . rejoice . . . honour

... slew him' – in order to show the inevitability of the actions following quickly one after another. He also ties words together through use of sound-puns or *paronomásia* with 'Censure me ... your senses', where the echo between 'censure' and 'senses' makes the audience alert to his main argument.

A central form of repetition-and-variation in the speech is *antithesis*, a powerful rhetorical device which sets contrasting ideas in close relation – 'not that I loved Caesar less, but that I loved Rome more'. Brutus uses this to set up one view against another, anticipating the thoughts of his audience and challenging them: 'You think I killed him because I didn't love him – you're wrong. I killed him because my love for Rome was greater than my love for Caesar.' He also uses antithesis again in line 7 as a rhetorical question (*erótema*). This antithesis sets loyalty to one man against loyalty to a city state, and he means us to see that the second love is more honourable than the first. Using the rhetorical question he forces his audience to consider the choice which he had to face and the ethical difficulties behind his action: 'Had you rather Caesar were living, and die all slaves, than that Caesar were dead, to live all free men?' In other words he is asking 'what choice was there?' and he answers it at the same time: 'This man had to die because he stood between Rome and freedom'.

It is also interesting to notice what kinds of rhetorical device are missing from Brutus's speech. He uses absolutely no figurative language, no active metaphors, no similes. His argument is full of abstract nouns (love, joy, virtue, honour) and he uses very active verbs (weep, rejoice, slay) to emphasise the ardour of his feelings and actions. All of these factors work to confirm the impression that this is a plain-speaking man of action, not overly contemplative or prone to poetic expressions. The dominant concepts in his speech are duty and moral integrity. However, it is the poetic and rhetorical register of Antony's speech that will persuade this crowd. Antony succeeds perhaps because he appeals to the passions and emotions of his audience, an audience who are already deeply moved by the news of the death of Caesar.

ACTIVITY 5:

It may be that Shakespeare's dramatic rhetoric now appeals to all kinds of new audiences, which the author could never have anticipated because he constructed his plays to appeal to quite different groups in his own period. His writing was already implicitly dialogical, constructed to reach out to a variety of people. His drama had to enter into dialogue with the mixed, often sceptical audiences of the popular theatre in Southwark, and simultaneously appeal to the monarch and Court elite across the river in Whitehall.

Construct a debate in response to Brutus's speech among the members of your group, developing what you think may have been the points of view of quite different spectators. For example:

- a young female servant in the Globe audience who has aspirations to 'better' herself, but is excluded from education and the means of advancement
- a young male apprentice, also in the Globe, with critical opinions of the way in which the Court dominates the political life of London and the nation
- by contrast, the opinions of a member of the Court establishment, close to the monarch: either a trusted councillor such as Robert Cecil, or a female member of one of the six 'great families' that dominated the court culture, such as Lucy Russell, Countess of Bedford, a patroness to many writers.

Using tropes: *Hamlet*

Here is another passage to consider.

Hamlet:
To be, or not to be – that is the question; (1)
Whether 'tis nobler in the mind to suffer
The slings and arrows of outrageous fortune,
Or to take arms against a sea of troubles
And by opposing end them. To die, to sleep – (5)
No more – and by a sleep to say we end
The heartache and the thousand natural shocks
That flesh is heir to. 'Tis a consummation
Devoutly to be wished. To die, to sleep –
To sleep – perchance to dream. Ay, there's the rub. (10)
For in that sleep of death what dreams may come,
When we have shuffled off this mortal coil* [tangled skein]
Must give us pause. There's the respect
That makes calamity of so long life.
For who would bear the whips and scorns of time, (15)
Th'oppressor's wrong, the proud man's contumely,* [reproach]
The pangs of despised love, the law's delay,
The insolence of office, and the spurns
That patient merit of th'unworthy takes,
When he himself might his quietus* make (20) [resolve a debt]
With a bare bodkin*? Who would fardels* bear, [dagger; burdens]
To grunt and sweat under a weary life,
But that the dread of something after death,
The undiscovered country, from whose bourn* [border]
No traveller returns, puzzles the will, (25)
And makes us rather bear those ills we have
Than fly to others that we know not of?
Thus conscience does make cowards of us all;
And thus the native hue of resolution

Is sicklied o'er with the pale cast of thought, (30)
And enterprises of great pitch and moment
With this regard their currents turn awry
And lose the name of action.

(*Hamlet* 3.1.56–88; Shakespeare 1996: 124–5)

ACTIVITY 6:

Using the discussion of Brutus's speech from *Julius Caesar* as a starting point, analyse the use of rhetoric in the 'To be or not to be' soliloquy from *Hamlet*. If you are working alone, break down the soliloquy into question and answer components in order to investigate its construction. If you are working in groups, explore the construction of argument by sharing out the soliloquy among different speakers in your group: this dramatises the question-and-answer inner dialogue that Hamlet is holding with himself. Then compare how different groups have divided the speech by performing your group-soliloquies to each other.

- How is the argument structured? Does it fall into blocks or sections of argument? Where are the breaks and changes of direction? What are the main claims or counter-claims of each section?
- Identify some rhetorical tropes and the ways in which they are used in the speech.
- Summarise the argument that Hamlet is making in modern English staying as close to the original as possible.
- Is the speech written in blank verse or prose? Why is it composed in this particular mode? To whom is this soliloquy addressed? How effective is the rhetorical appeal?

ACTIVITY 7:

Watch a film version of the speech such as Mel Gibson's performance in Franco Zeffirelli's *Hamlet* (1991) or Kenneth Branagh's full-text film (1997). To gain some sense of how radically performance expectations change over the decades, you could compare these recent versions of the play with Laurence Olivier's performance from 1948. Which do you prefer and why? Consider the following questions. Does the film format help or hinder the delivery of this speech? In your opinion, how well do Gibson, Branagh or Olivier deliver their versions of the speech? How do they handle the rhetorical structure and tropes of the argument?

ACTIVITY 8:

Write a letter (in prose or blank verse) addressed to the Prince from one of the following roles: Ophelia, Gertrude, 'old' Hamlet, Horatio, Claudius. Using as many of the rhetorical conventions as you can, try to persuade Hamlet from your adopted character's point of view that he is making a mistake by being so consumed with despair. Afterwards write a short analysis of your letter which identifies the rhetorical conventions you have used.

Brutus chose to speak to the Roman plebeians in prose as a strategic rhetorical choice. Prince Hamlet, by contrast, here speaks in *blank verse*, which is unrhymed five-stress ('iambic pentameter') poetry. In Shakespeare's plays this form of verse tends to be used by characters with high social status. Although critics have often considered that this soliloquy is 'incoherent' and have taken it as evidence of Hamlet's growing madness, the rhetorical structure of the speech is quite clear in terms of traditional rhetoric. First, Hamlet poses a question which the rest of the speech will answer. Having set himself the question he begins to 'brainstorm' it (*'invention'*, lines 1–5). Second, he argues the first *thesis*, or *'disposition'*, in lines 5–9. Third, he counters this first answer with an opposing answer (which we call an *antithesis*) in lines 9–14. This is followed by two confirming rhetorical questions, lines 15–27. Finally he concludes with a *synthesis* in lines 28–30. So Hamlet, far from being out of control, is actually using the rhetorical debating techniques of the universities and Inns of Court (the 'postgraduate institutions' of Renaissance England) by posing a *'quaestio'* which had to be evaluated for and against. Like all good Renaissance arguments, it is a variation on a thoroughly traditional topic – as old as St Augustine's thoughts in *On Free Will*: 'It is not because I would rather be unhappy than not be at all, that I am unwilling to die, but for fear that after death I may be still more unhappy' (see Shakespeare 1982: 489).

Hamlet's soliloquy is an excellent demonstration of the way in which 'internal' dialogue can also become 'external' through the involvement of the audience within the dynamic of its questions and answers. Line 1 is the most famous *erótema* (rhetorical question) in literature. Line 3 uses personification (*prosopopóeia*) to portray fortune or life as an aggressor armed with slings and arrows. Line 4 continues to demonstrate the hopelessness of his situation by using the most infamous mixed metaphor in literature – who would try to use weapons against the sea? Well, you might if you were a Celtic warrior demonstrating conscious heroism. Shakespeare, again in true Renaissance fashion, is quoting an authority: 'as the Celts take up their arms to go to meet the waves' (Aristotle, *Nichomachean Ethics* 3.7; Shakespeare 1982: 491). And this is precisely the difficulty that Hamlet suffers – is there any point in trying to do anything when life is so relentlessly tragic? Hamlet uses *hypérbole* (exaggeration) in line 7 to emphasise again the enormity of the suffering that 'flesh is heir to', and 'flesh' here represents 'people' so is an example of *synécdoche*, a part representing the whole.

The tight rhetorical structure (question, thesis, antithesis, synthesis), the use of rhetorical questions to signal new stages in the thought processes, and the use of metaphor and personification to emphasise and visualise the hopelessness of Hamlet's situation all indicate the vital influence of rhetoric on Hamlet's thinking – and on Shakespeare's writing. This again demonstrates the very public nature of this thought and speech on the Renaissance stage. Modern productions of the play have tended to emphasise the fragile psychology of Hamlet by playing the speech as a tortured, even incoherent meditation. But given the understanding of rhetoric as an essentially public form of argument it is likely that the actors who played Hamlet in Shakespeare's own time performed the anguished soliloquy as a shared conversation with their audiences, and would have stood front-of-stage, eyeballing individual spectators and riveting their attention through the rhetorical address. And those members of the audience who had attended grammar schools or university would have been keenly aware of the controlled rhetorical structures within the speech.

ACTIVITY 9:

Now perform sharply contrasting versions of the soliloquy. The first should be in 'sixteenth-century' style, emphasising the rhetorical address direct to an audience which is invited to share the dilemmas posed within the speech. In this delivery try to emphasise the metrical organisation of the speech by paying attention to the rhythm and metre of the blank verse. By contrast, deliver the soliloquy in a more 'naturalistic' twentieth-century style which represents the character as hopelessly lost within a private catastrophe (think, for example, of Marlon Brando's performance of Kurtz in Francis Ford Copolla's *Heart of Darkness*). Try to deliver this version of the speech more prosaically and naturalistically. Try and assess your speech using the Criteria for Oral Assessment in the Appendix. If you are working in groups, give each other constructive feedback on your performances based on these Criteria. Which approach works best? What different kinds of question do they raise about the Prince and his dilemma? Are the two versions absolutely opposed in their methods and the kinds of performance they generate?

ACTIVITY 10:

Take a well-known character from a soap opera or film and write (or record on audio-tape) a short dramatic monologue in which the character talks aloud to him or herself about a predicament. Try to create a strong rhetorical structure for the series of arguments and counter-arguments the character will express. You will also need to make the piece dramatically effective. Draft and redraft (or re-record) the piece several times until it is polished. Write a short commentary on your piece, identifying the rhetorical devices you used and analysing any problems you encountered, or issues you felt the activity raised.

Summary

In this chapter we have introduced you to:

- politics, rhetoric and class in Shakespearean England
- rhetoric in the grammar schools
- rhetoric in *Romeo and Juliet*
- rhetorical tropes
- rhetoric in *Julius Caesar*
- rhetoric in *Hamlet*.

References

Baxandall, Michael (1971) *Giotto and the Orators: Humanist Observers of Painting in Italy and the Discovery of Pictorial Composition*. Oxford: Clarendon Press.

Cicero (1949) *De inventione* (On Invention), trans. H.M. Hubbell. London: Heinemann.

Jonson, Ben (1995) *Timber or Discoveries*, ed. Ian Donaldson. Oxford: Oxford University Press.

Mack, Peter (ed.) (1994) *Renaissance Rhetoric*. Basingstoke: Macmillan.

Pope, Rob (1998) *The English Studies Book*. London: Routledge.

Puttenham, George (1968) *The Arte of English Poesie* [1589]. London: Scolar Press.

Shakespeare, William (1982) *Hamlet*, ed. Harold Jenkins. London: Methuen.

Shakespeare, William (1984) *Romeo and Juliet*, ed. G. Blakemore Evans. Cambridge: Cambridge University Press.

Shakespeare, William (1986) *Julius Caesar* in *The Complete Works*, ed. Stanley Wells and Gary Taylor. Oxford: Clarendon Press.

Shakespeare, William (1991) *The Second Part of King Henry VI*, ed. Michael Hattaway. Cambridge: Cambridge University Press.

Shakespeare, William (1996) *Hamlet*, ed. T.J.B. Spencer with an introduction by Anne Barton. London: Penguin.

Tannen, Deborah (1992) *You Just Don't Understand: Women and Men in Conversation*. London: Virago.

Wheale, Nigel (1999) *Writing and Society. Literacy, Print and Politics, Britain 1590–1660*. London: Routledge.

CHAPTER 4

Everyday rhetorics

Simon Featherstone

The forms of rhetoric that we have been discussing in the last two chapters might seem remote from our everyday experience for contemporary Britain tends to be wary of rhetorical language. In fact, the very term has changed its significance to reflect this mistrust, with *Chambers Dictionary* giving a main definition of 'rhetorical' as 'inflated, over-elaborate or insincere in style'. Walter Ong, in his definitive study of the relationship of speaking and writing, sees this as part of a wider historical change in education and society that began in the eighteenth century: 'The three R's reading, 'riting, and 'rithmatic – representing an essentially non-rhetorical, bookish, commercial and domestic education, gradually took over from the traditional orally-grounded, heroic, agonistic education that had generally prepared young men in the past for teaching and professional, ecclesiastical, or political public service' (Ong 1982: 116). However, the fading of traditional rhetorical practice does not mean that contemporary culture is unrhetorical. Forms of persuasion proliferate, and whilst their language may not be immediately identifiable as the kind of rhetoric described in the last chapter, they often use similar strategies. This chapter will survey four areas of contemporary rhetoric. We will see how traditional forms of speaking have survived in some formal public contexts, how new versions of rhetoric have evolved in an increasingly commercial society, how rhetoric remains fundamental to personal expression through story-telling, and how forms of rhetoric have developed in other English-speaking cultures.

Classical rhetoric has survived longest in its archaic forms in the public rituals of the professions to which Ong refers – in parliamentary procedures and speeches, the church sermon, the lecture, and the courtroom. Each of these has, or had, its own discourse, rooted in rhetorical tradition, that defined its power in a public display of language and ritual. However, recent cultural and technological changes have significantly modified these rhetorics. The demands of television, inside and outside the Houses of Parliament, are for brief 'sound-bites' rather than lengthy, elaborately constructed speeches. The church sermon has similarly undergone radical change in the face of rapid secularisation. The classical styles of argument that saturated the performances of the great Anglican preachers, from John Donne to Charles Wesley, have been replaced by a more prosaic, message-based approach. One recent preaching handbook, for example, poses the problem of 'talking to people whose minds are frequently informed by television, videos, computer games and the Internet . . . No longer are people learning primarily through seeing or hearing words and ideas', and it goes on to offer brief anecdotes of everyday life to meet this challenge (Twelftree 1996: 9).

Rhetoric in the criminal court

The criminal court, founded on the adversarial model of ancient Rome, is perhaps the civic arena where classical rhetoric is most fully preserved, though even here there are strong pressures for change. Trials are normally conducted with defence and prosecution lawyers attempting to persuade an impartial jury of the innocence or guilt of the accused by questioning witnesses, interpreting evidence and addressing the jury directly with their 'narrative' of the case. 'Trials are linguistic events', writes John Gibbons (1994: 3), and the command of the discourse of law and its adequate performance in the courtroom 'theatre' is obviously crucial to the outcome. In such a performance there is the risk that the inequalities of linguistic power between those that command the appropriate rhetoric (the judge and lawyers) and those that don't (usually the defendants, witnesses and jury) will lead to injustice. In the circumstances of a trial, lack of rhetorical skill, and of knowledge of appropriate syntax and lexis, can have serious consequences. As John Gibbons writes, the 'adversarial approach, by its very nature, is likely to discredit those who are less articulate in legal language, or easily intimidated' (1994: 197). Mark Brennan gives an example of the style of questioning that would probably intimidate a defendant (in this case a fifteen-year-old boy): 'Would it be incorrect to suggest that it was not so much a tripping· but because of the state of inebriation of yourself, that you fell over?' (1994: 216). The question could be phrased as 'Did you fall over because you were drunk?', but the lawyer introduces complex syntax, a negative construction and a formal register. Even if the boy knew that 'inebriation' meant drunkenness, the elaborate syntax would make the question difficult to understand, and his response uncertain and so more likely to be unconvincing.

There have been occasions, though, where participants in a trial have exploited the contrast between legal rhetoric and everyday speech in order to reverse the power structure defined by Gibbons. One such case was the trial of Pat Pottle at the Old Bailey in 1991. Pottle, along with Michael

Randle, was tried for aiding the escape from prison of George Blake, who was convicted of spying for the USSR. The escape took place in the 1960s, and neither of the defendants was himself an agent – they were in prison for acts of civil disobedience. They agreed to help Blake because they considered his sentence of forty-two years inhumane. Although police had known about their involvement since at least the 1970s, the prosecution was only made when Pottle wrote a book that acknowledged his part in the escape. Pottle conducted his own defence, and what follows is part of his final address to the jury. Throughout the trial he didn't deny what he had done, and here he appeals to the jury to ignore the technicalities of law and consider the issue of justice: was it right to prosecute after so long; was Blake's sentence just; was a prosecution justified in the light of the generous treatment of other known spies, such as Sir Anthony Blunt, once the curator of the Queen's art collection? He and his co-defendant were acquitted.

This the only opportunity I have of speaking directly to you. Sitting in the jury box must be boring and frustrating. If it is any consolation to you, I can assure you it beats sitting in the dock. Let's open the windows, let the fresh air in, and blow away the cobwebs. Let common sense, for once, be champion over legal technicalities.

This prosecution has come about because 110 MPs signed a motion calling for our prosecution – and because of a threat of a private prosecution from the inaptly named Freedom Association. We do not deny the things we are accused of doing. Not only do we not deny it, we say it was the right thing to do.

Your task would be a lot easier if this were a simple case of guilt or innocence, but it is not. It is a case of right and wrong. It is a case of politics, a case of how governments lie, cheat and manipulate, and then cover their tracks in a smokescreen of official secrecy.

This is not just a case of a man given an inhuman sentence and of us freeing him. This is a political trial . . .

The judge has ruled our reasons for freeing George to be irrelevant. In law, he says, these people have no defence. You have no choice but to find them guilty. I disagree with the judge. The idea of a jury system is that you can look at the whole case, not just the legal mumbo-jumbo. You are twelve independent people.

Unlike most judges you exist in the ordinary world of everyday life. You are able to use your common sense and humanity and not have your hands and minds tied by legal technicalities. Common sense must tell you that our reasons for helping to free George from prison must be relevant. If you accept the narrow legal position that the judge may direct you to make, you diminish your own roles as jurors.

The moral indignation about George's work for the Russians is something I completely agree with. But moral outrage is only genuine when applied to both sides. Have our values become so perverted that we only claim moral outrage at the other side's activities and not our own?

What George did for British intelligence and the KGB was wrong – we have never tried to justify it nor whitewash it. But espionage is a dirty business, where rumour becomes fact and fact becomes fiction. The individuals involved in it are exploiters and in turn exploited. Even when caught they can still be used as international pawns in a game, some to be swapped, some to be given immunity, and the unlucky ones left to rot in prison. No one who supports this kind of thing can hold their heads up high.

What did George do that sets him apart from other spies uncovered at that time? He was not really British, was he? Not of the old school, not one of us. Deep down he was a foreigner, and half Jewish to boot. He was never part of that privileged undergraduate set at Cambridge in the 1930s. Not like dear old Kim [Philby – head of MI6, who was also a Soviet agent], who was offered immunity, or dear old Anthony [Blunt], who was not only given immunity but allowed to continue his work as Surveyor of the Queen's Pictures.

A secret trial, a vicious sentence of 42 years, a secret appeal – is this democracy in action? Is this open justice? Are we not becoming the very thing we condemn?

George was no threat to you, me, or our children. He had been caught spying for the Russians, just as they had caught people spying for the West. His usefulness was over, his spying activities at an end. What purpose was served by giving him such a sentence? It was, in the words of Lord Hutchinson: 'so inhuman that it is alien to all the principles by which a civilised country should treat its subjects'.

When the Government and its judges allow themselves to be dictated to by mob hysteria you end up with a society whose laws and penal institutions are based on revenge and nothing else.

In the end it comes down to this: a fellow human being asked for help. That help meant breaking the law. I feel no shame in having done so, but I would have felt great shame had I turned down George's request for help.

Yes, I helped George Blake escape. I did it for purely humanitarian reasons. I think we were right to do so. I would do it again. I have no apologies to make and no regrets.

I will finish by quoting Bertrand Russell: 'Remember your humanity; forget the rest.'

(*The Guardian*, 27 June 1991: 21)

ACTIVITY 1:

Consider Pottle's approach to this crucial speech – if found guilty he could have spent many years in prison. In what ways is he deliberately non-rhetorical? Are there ways in which the speech *is* rhetorical? Write a short analysis of the speech, considering how Pottle draws on or challenges rhetorical conventions to persuade his audience of his point of view. If you are working in groups, elect a chair or foreperson of the jury. Discuss Pottle's speech. What kind of responses do you think he is trying to achieve? What specific parts of the speech would elicit such responses? Would you acquit Pottle and his co-defendant? If so, why? If not, why not? Write up a short report.

Rhetoric is everywhere

The rhetoric of law is a discursive system that most of us will only encounter occasionally, if we're lucky. But other survivals of old rhetoric are more firmly embedded in the culture of everyday life. Whilst Britain is an increasingly secular and vernacular society, the need to mark significant occasions and rites of passage rhetorically, by formal public statement, is still strong. Gatherings to celebrate birthdays, engagements, retirements, funerals and anniversaries require speeches to be made, which, although they are often humorous, are noticeably formal in their construction and performance. The ongoing *need* for rhetoric has many manifestations, one of which is the use of poetry by people who may not otherwise pay much attention to literature at all. The rhyming verses in traditional birthday cards and in death notices in local newspapers are examples of this. Another was provided by a driver on a Birmingham to Cambridge train. On entering Cambridge he announced that this was his last journey before retirement, and to mark it he had written a poem, which he proceeded to read. It was funny and sad, and written in carefully metrical rhyming couplets. A further example of the continuing public use of poetic rhetoric occurred in a village in Wales. The closure of the only pub in the late 1980s was followed by the appearance of several anonymous poems of protest and lament posted up at strategic points of the village. The poems galvanised local feeling into a successful campaign to reopen the pub, where the poems are now displayed on the wall. Carefully argued letters to the local newspaper probably wouldn't have had the same effect as these self-consciously rhetorical and public 'demonstrations' of feeling.

Perhaps the most frequent encounter of the ordinary with the rhetorical occurs at weddings, however. After the religious or civil rhetoric of the ceremony, participants are usually expected to engage in their own rhetorical acts. The 'traditional' order of speeches is fixed, and, as most people have probably witnessed, the occasion can expose unease with the linguistic conventions and performative demands of wedding rhetoric – as well as sometimes revealing some unexpected rhetorical resources. The rhetoric of wedding speeches is sufficiently challenging to have resulted in a large number of 'How To Speak' books, which provide interesting guides to the conventions and dangers of such performances. Those dangers have always been a rich source of material for comedians able to exploit the rhetorical mistakes and embarrassments that the pressure of formal speeches provoke (one of the most successful British films of recent years, *Four Weddings and a Funeral* (1994), was organised around such performances). What follows is an example of a father-of-the-bride speech taken from Angela Lansbury's *Wedding Speeches and Toasts* (1988), and an extract from the comedian Rowan Atkinson's stage act which featured parodies of three wedding-day speeches, including, as here, one by the bride's father.

Speech 1
Reverend Brown, Ladies and Gentlemen, all my guests, I cannot tell you how pleased I am today to see my daughter Annabelle looking so radiantly happy, as she begins life as the wife of Steven. My wife and I do not feel that we are losing Annabelle, but entrusting her to Steven's good care. During the last few months as we have got to know him better, he has shown himself to be exactly the sort of person we had hoped Annabelle would marry – charming, sincere, reliable – with a clear idea of what he wants from life and how to achieve it. I know that his many friends and family, as well as those who have only recently met him, think that this must be one of those marriages that are made in heaven, and will want to join me in wishing Steven and Annabelle a long and happy married life together. So please stand and raise your glasses, and drink to the health and happiness of Annabelle and Steven.

(Lansbury 1988: 37–8)

Speech 2
Ladies and gentlemen, and friends of my daughter, there comes a time in every wedding reception when the man who paid for the damn thing is allowed to speak a word or two of his own. And I should like to speak much as my wife sang in the service that we've all just (*pause*) enjoyed, with no real notes. Primarily, I'd like to take this opportunity, pissed as I may be, to say a word or two about Martin. As far as I'm concerned, my daughter could not have chosen a more delightful, charming, witty, responsible, wealthy – let's not deny it – well-placed, good-looking and fertile young man than Martin as her husband. And I therefore ask the question: why the hell did she marry Gerald instead?

(Atkinson 1995)

ACTIVITY 2:

Read through the speeches and discuss the following questions in your groups. What rhetorical features do you notice? What is the purpose of the first speech? What rules of language and values are breached in Atkinson's parody? Make some notes in preparation for writing the opening of your own best man/woman speech (Activity 3).

ACTIVITY 3:

Now write the beginning of a best man/woman speech for a friend, a public personality, or if you are working with others, a member of your group. Define the conventions that you will need to follow. Rehearse your speech and practise performing it. If you have time, complete the speech.

Rhetoric in selling

So far we have been considering everyday encounters with surviving forms of classical rhetoric, and the questions of convention, power and performance that they raise. Other forms of rhetoric, though, permeate our culture, entering our language and structuring our perception of the world. Arguably the most influential of these in the last forty years is that of selling. We live in a world that is saturated with language, image and performance via TV, radio, newspapers, hoardings and shops, persuading us to think about products and issues in certain ways, and to buy or commit ourselves to them. So relentless is the presence of advertising, in fact, that we filter out many of its messages, provoking even more advertisements to re-sensitise us to their presence. But however sophisticated advertisements and selling techniques have become, their process is grounded in the strategy of classical rhetoric. As Patrick Ellis expresses it in *Who Dares Sells*, 'What is required is sales talk with an objective, structured with logical and emotional appeal' (Ellis 1992: 157), a definition of rhetoric with which Aristotle and Cicero might agree. The numerous books on selling practice, particularly those concerned with person-to-person selling, are really modern rhetorical primers. They attempt to train their readers in clarifying objectives, structuring ideas and arguments, thinking about their audience/customers, selecting the most appropriate vocabulary, and overcoming potential obstacles – all the things, in fact, that this book deals with in preparation for presentations and debates. Language and its rhetorical possibilities are central to the concerns of sales training, far more so, in fact, than any technical knowledge or psychological insight. In *How to Master the Art of Selling*, for example, Tom Hopkins spends a lengthy chapter on dealing with linguistic connotation, particularly what he calls 'rejection words', which are defined as 'any term that triggers fear, or reminds prospects [prospective customers] that you are trying to sell to them' (Hopkins 1994: 65). Rejection words include 'cost', 'monthly payment', 'contract', 'buy' and 'sign', and it is part of the salesman's task to redefine this negative discourse. So Hopkins suggests that 'sign the contract' becomes in salesperson–customer dialogue 'authorize the agreement', and a sentence such as 'When you buy our product, you'll be happy with it' becomes 'When you own our product, you'll be happy with it'. In the ideology of selling, everybody wants to own, but nobody wants to buy, and so the rhetoric of the salesperson must persuade potential customers of the advantages of ownership.

The act of selling, then, is a linguistic act of persuasion, and like the other rhetorical acts that we have considered so far, it is a linguistic performance, too. It takes place in a particular place, at a particular time, and is directed to a particular (and probably sceptical) audience. The seller's craft lies in adapting the language to the circumstances. Colin Clark and Trevor Pinch's study *The Hard Sell* (1995) examines the techniques of street- and market-traders, the most direct dealers in the public rhetoric of selling, and they find in their patter identifiable rhetorical strategies, a developed sense of performance and an anticipation and reading of their fluid and transient audience. Here is one example of their rhetoric taken from a market sock-seller:

> You'll be able to keep them for ten years, maybe twenty years. You're gonna give them to your children and your children will give them to your grandchildren. Have a look madam.
> [customer examines socks]
> Don't forget to see your solicitor after you buy these. Don't forget to see your solicitor about changing your inheritance.

> (Clark and Pinch 1995: 31)

This is street *parison* and *hyperbole* (see previous chapter), by which the socks become heirlooms and the sock-seller an adviser on inheritance law. As Clark and Pinch point out, though, these extravagant claims are not meant seriously, and their comedy is part of the rhetorical strategy: 'they are meant to entertain the crowd as well as deal with the difficult task of trying to sell goods on a street market' (31). In such speech acts the rhetoric is parodying its own claims; we know it is extravagant, but part of the seller's persuasiveness is in allowing us to enjoy that knowledge. Such ironic games are necessary for the effectiveness of rhetoric in an anti-rhetorical age.

ACTIVITY 4:

On your own or in pairs, draft a 'patter act' to sell something in a market. Remember market selling is stylised and playful, working by repetition and extravagance as well as by appealing to people's love of a bargain. Write a short commentary on the use of rhetoric in your street-selling act.

Alternatively, find a local market in your area and listen to the street-sellers in performance. Transcribe some of the patter and write up a short report on one particular street-selling style and techniques including dialogue and banter with the audience. Include a commentary on the audience response.

As we have emphasised throughout this book, rhetoric works in specific circumstances of time, place and culture, and advertising is particularly attuned to the implications of its own moment. Guy Cook, in *The Discourse of Advertising*, suggests that 'ads have no voice of their own . . . they are a fluctuating and unstable mixture of the voices around them, constantly transmuting and recombining' (Cook 1992: 217), their persuasive power being short-lived and constantly in need of renewal. A 1930s advertisement for telephones, for example, in which the Post-Master General is pictured saying 'Fears and doubts thrive well in the home where the telephone is not' alongside a photograph of a man worrying about his absent wife, could no longer be effective (though its quaintness of phrasing and the potential comedy of the situation might mean it could be used ironically by current advertisers) (see Turner 1952: 198). Although in some contexts advertising has remained consistently direct and 'traditional' in its form and language – on commercial local radio, for example – most advertising is constantly striving for novelty, for effective and striking rhetorical devices which will overcome the 'fatigue' of audiences over-exposed to advertising. In recent years explicit language of persuasion has been removed from many advertisements, leaving only images, the name of a product and a surrounding 'drama' that entertains the viewer. 'The point', as Sean Brierley suggests, 'is not to appear to be selling at all . . . The idea is that consumers are left thinking that they are not being manipulated and that they are free to make up their own minds' (Brierley 1995: 161). In other advertisements the reverse occurs, and the process of persuasion is made very explicit and therefore playfully ironic. Thus a product might be advertised by an actor dressed as a pseudo-Kray twin gangster saying 'Buy it now – or else', a statement that simultaneously sends up and delivers the message of the advertisement. In advertisements that can't use comedy, the recent tendency is for a very short, blackly ironic sentence to be used; messages about, for example, drink driving or child neglect are no longer delivered as sentimental or sentencious arguments, but as tough, judgmental statements.

ACTIVITY 5:

Choose two or three of the old advertisements shown. Make notes on the rhetorical features you notice and how you think they are used to appeal to each advert's contemporary audience. Rewrite the advertisements in ways which are more suitable for our contemporary culture. For each one provide a short commentary explaining the reasons for the changes that you have made in your rewriting. If you are working in groups, circulate your new version within your group for feedback.

Advertisement 1 Newspaper advertisement for Eno's 'Fruit Salt', 1890

No stale traces
to menace health after

VIM's *DOUBLE* ACTION CLEANSING

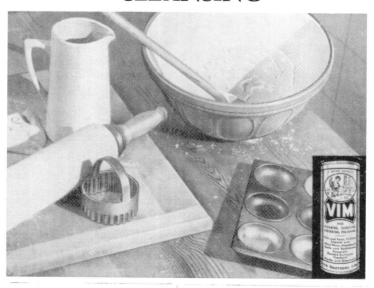

It you look closely you will see that even *smooth* woodwork has furrows. These, clogged with dirt and food scraps, are danger points in any kitchen. Double Action Vim gives protection here.

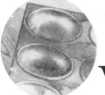

In the pitted surfaces of cooking pans particles decay and taint the food. Kitchen utensils must be kept hygienic. Let Vim do that.

IN the ordinary way of cleaning up after cooking many atoms of food find hiding places. This can be a real danger, as science shows, for these atoms may become poisonous and taint the food. To prevent this, Vim was made with Double Action cleansing properties. It enables you, without extra work, to keep utensils and surfaces really clean and healthy.

For Vim not only loosens the fragments from the surface but absorbs them, surrounds them, and allows you to wipe them clean away. A rinse or wipe over after a rub with Vim leaves a really hygienic cleanliness.

VIM *(1) LOOSENS THE DIRT*
(2) THEN ABSORBS IT

A LEVER PRODUCT

V 498 206-89

Advertisement 2 Poster advertisement for Vim, 1935

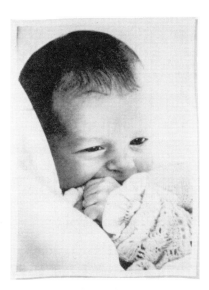

If you've just had your first baby, what are you to believe?

Young mothers are great targets for well meant advice. It comes from all directions. At best it's confusing; at worst it could be harmful.

For instance, you'll probably hear a lot of opinions expressed on the question of baby's first solids. And here it's important that you don't take chances. The rule is—listen only to experts. To people who really understand babies, like your clinic and your doctor—and Heinz.

When you choose Heinz Baby Foods you choose security—for yourself and for baby. Heinz Baby Foods are full of natural goodness. Little mouths open wide and willingly for the delicious flavours.

You'll soon discover baby's personal favourites from among Heinz 72 varieties.

Gradually build up to a varied and balanced diet (Heinz booklet "From Milk to Mixed Diet" will tell you how). Put your trust in Heinz. Then you, and baby, can't go wrong.

For your copy of "From Milk to Mixed Diet" write to Susan Baxter, Baby Foods Advisory Service, H. J. Heinz Co. Ltd., Hayes Park, Hayes, Middlesex.

There just isn't anything better for your baby than

Heinz Baby Foods

38

Advertisement 3 Magazine advertisement for Heinz Baby Food, 1966

What's a nice girl like this doing in the Army?

The Army – what kind of job is that for a girl with looks, personality and intelligence?

To the girl in the photograph, it's a very challenging and rewarding one. For Christine Cardwell is a Second Lieutenant in the Women's Royal Army Corps.

If that surprises you, perhaps you don't know as much about the Army as you think. Like any large company or organisation, the Army does expect you to be responsible; to carry out instructions; to respect your bosses; to dress appropriately, and be in on time. But the Army of today is new in every sense of the word, and for a true perspective on it, look at the girls who've joined.

There's nothing unfeminine or old-fashioned about Christine Cardwell. She's an administrator and personnel manager with a regiment of the Royal Artillery – to use the Army jargon, she's the Assistant Adjutant. Like most WRAC officers, she works alongside the men of the Army; basically her concern is always with soldiers and servicewomen.

Whether they're working with artillery, supplies, computers or communications; whether in England, Germany, Cyprus or Hong Kong, everyone in the Army needs to be able to work well with people. Because this doesn't come easily to everyone, Army training is very important.

Christine's first posting, as a nineteen year old, put her in charge of around fifty servicewomen, many older than herself. Eight months' officer training had given her the self-confidence to cope.

Responsibility and challenge are by no means all the Army offers. Christine has found more friends here than almost any other job could provide. She's also found a fiancé. And the time and opportunity to learn ski-ing and parachuting. Today, officers start on £2,555 a year. You can join for as little as two years on a Short Service Commission.

To make up your own mind about the challenge of the Army, find out more by writing to Lt. Col. Barbara Laverack M.B.E., WRAC Officer Entry, CO/W188A, Lansdowne House, Berkeley Square, London W1X 6AA.

WRAC Officer

**The New Army.
The challenge you need.**

168

Advertisement 4 Magazine army recruitment advertisement, 1976

As writers on advertising have suggested, advertising copy draws on many of the rhetorical devices conventionally associated with literature and oratory (see, for example, Brierley 1995: 173–87). It is perhaps not surprising, therefore, that some influential contemporary writers have spent time in the industries of advertising and selling – Fay Weldon and Salman Rushdie to name just two. Another is the American dramatist David Mamet, whose play *Glengarry Glen Ross* (1984) concerns the attempts of real estate salesmen to offload worthless land in Florida. Mamet is interested both in the moral and political meanings of selling in America, and in exploiting for dramatic effect the rhetorical performances of selling. Perhaps the most striking scene in the play takes place in a bar where we see the salesman, Roma, apparently engaged in casual conversation with a stranger, Lingk. This is the first time that the audience has encountered either character and, like Lingk, we listen to Roma's apparently confessional speech about sex and a personal philosophy of resolute decision-making and trusting to instincts. By the end of the speech, however, we come to realise that the monologue has been a sales pitch, moving ever closer to the issue of buying the Glengarry Glen Ross lands. The unrhetorical 'honesty' of the confession is the strategy of the sale. This is the final part of the scene:

Roma: . . . Stocks, bonds, objects of art, real estate. Now: what are they? (*Pause.*) An opportunity. To what? To make money? Perhaps. To *lose* money? Perhaps. To 'indulge' and to 'learn' about ourselves? Perhaps. *So fucking what? What isn't?* They're an *opportunity*. That's all. They're an *event*. A guy comes up to you, you make a call, you send in a brochure, it doesn't matter, 'There these *properties* I'd like for you to see.' What does it mean? What you *want* it to mean. (*Pause.*) Money? (*Pause.*) If that's what it signifies to you. Security? (*Pause.*) Comfort? 'Some schmuck wants to make a buck on me'; or, 'I feel a vibration *fate* is calling' . . . all it is is THINGS THAT HAPPEN TO YOU. (*Pause.*) That's all it is. How are they different? (*Pause.*) Some poor newly married guy gets run down by a cab. Some *busboy* wins the lottery . . . (*Pause.*) All it is, it's a carnival. What's special . . . what *draws* us . . . ? (*Pause.*) We're all different. (*Pause.*) We're not the same . . . (*Pause.*) We're not the same . . . Hmmm . . . (*Pause. Sighs.*) It's been a long day. (*Pause.*) What are you drinking?
Lingk: Gimlet.
Roma: Well, let's have a couple more. My name is Richard Roma. What's yours?
Lingk: Lingk. James Lingk.
Roma: James. I'm glad to meet you. (*They shake hands.*) I'm glad to meet you, James. (*Pause.*) I want to show you something. (*Pause.*) It might mean *nothing* to you . . . and it might not. I don't know. I don't know anymore. (*Pause. He takes out a small map and spreads it on the table.*) What is that? Florida. Glengarry Highlands. Florida. 'Florida. *Bullshit.*' And maybe that's

true; and that's what *I* said: but look *here*: What is this? This is a piece of land. Listen to what I'm going to tell you now:

(Mamet 1984: 25–6)

The American sales guru Tom Hopkins writes that '[s]eldom do people buy logically' (Hopkins 1994: 58), and Mamet's Roma here elevates (or debases) the act of selling to a conversation about the meaning of life, appealing to a stranger in a bar by a language that is *calculated* to appeal to such a man. Roma improvises a selling rhetoric from the apparently unlikely material of male bar talk. In its unlikeliness is its power, and Lingk buys the useless land. Through Roma's sale Mamet raises the question of whether in a society predicated on the hard sell, there can be any conversation that is entirely innocent of its rhetorical strategies.

ACTIVITY 6:

Write a radio script for an advertisement for any product or service of your choice using appropriate rhetorical devices. You have a maximum of one minute air-time. You should specify your chosen radio station and pitch your advertisement at that particular audience.

Rhetoric in story-telling

The everyday rhetoric that we have looked at so far has involved a deliberate use of discourses that can be designed and adapted to social objectives, whether it be securing a conviction in court, fulfilling the conventional demands of a wedding ceremony or selling land to an unlucky 'prospect'. Different kinds of negotiations lie behind the fourth example of everyday rhetoric that we will consider, that of story-telling. Telling stories doesn't seem as formal or as deliberated as the other rhetorical acts that we have examined, but it is fundamental to our sense of individual and social identity. Story-telling as a public act of oratory was a central feature of oral cultures, and allowed cultures without writing to collectively remember the community's histories, beliefs and knowledge. The history of writing, printing, cinema and video is the history of the privatisation of the story, something encapsulated by the silent reading of a novel, an act unimaginable in any culture until the late eighteenth century. Nevertheless, although formal sessions of story-telling, between adults at least, are relatively rare in mainstream British culture, the narrative impulse, the need to create and perform stories about ourselves and the world in which we live, remains. It is a need that has been recognised by the twentieth-century practice and discourse of psychoanalysis and counselling, in which treatment is founded upon the telling of an individual's stories. For the therapist, the only access to his/her clients' problems is the narratives and their telling. Such stories, as the therapist David Howe points out, concern people's remaking and interpretation of their lives. 'The past is not a fixed thing, lying somewhere deep in the memory banks of the brain simply to be recovered by some archaeologist of the mind', he writes. 'People rework their past experiences as they tell their tale . . . the individual *reconstructs* her past rather than *recovers* it' (Howe 1993: 155).

Telling stories about ourselves and others is how we know about ourselves and how we communicate our knowledge publicly, even if only to friends and colleagues: everyone is their own story-teller. But story-telling also has its expert ordinary practitioners. We all know good story-tellers who can hold our attention with a tale about little or nothing, or who can make us laugh with a story that becomes very ordinary when we try to re-tell it later. The German cultural theorist Walter Benjamin called this kind of everyday story-teller a craftsman whose task is to 'fashion the raw material of experience, his own and that of others, in a solid, useful, and unique way' (Benjamin 1973: 108). Such people may perform in the kitchen, the pub or the workplace, but they do so as rhetoricians whether they know it in those terms or not, and however natural and improvised their story might sound. A good story-teller shapes and performs his/her narrative material in order to hold a particular audience's attention, using the available resources of language, sound and body to elicit the desired response, be it laughter, fear, shock or mystification. The following story, told in the 1970s by Jack Hill, a retired miner from Derbyshire, suggests some of these skills in action.

> That were another good time when I went home from the pit one day, me dad says, 'Eh up Johnny', he says, 'I want you to go with me'. I said, 'Where?' He says, 'To Codnor' – or Kimberley, something like that it were. 'I've got a job to do. A woman wants a piano shifting.' I said, 'Ew'. I says, 'All right. I'll have a bit of tea and go with you.' And it was summertime, like. So we started off – I think it was Kimberley as we'd got to fetch it from and loaded the piano up and me dad was supposed to – I don't know whether he were drunk or what – he was supposed to have fastened it down as it couldn't shift. Well, we put it on the horse and barrow – they were barrows in them days, you know, not like drays, barrows they were [two-wheeled carts]. And we'd got a horse in the shafts – weren't a very heavy horse. Any road, we started from Kimberley and I thought me dad had tethered this here down tightly like. And we comes towards Newton's Hill, and you know the bridge at the top of there, well you went up first didn't you, and then just quick turned over the bridge, the cut [canal] bridge. Well, we went up this side, well, when we were going up this side the bloody piano started slipping back and of course by the time we'd got onto brow, the weight of the piano was on the back of the cart and it picked the horse up off the floor. And I dived off the bloody cart

I did mysen, and my dad, he were a cripple – he couldna. And it were going down Newton's Hill, and he were pulling the reins this road and that road, and he corrected himself, he corrected the horse – and it were hung up in the air like that. Well, when we gets to the bottom of the hill I comes running after them like, there were two colliers going to work, and they steadied it – it'd have killed him. And they steadied it down and the horse came back to the floor like. They hutched the piano up again and it brought the horse down to the floor again, see. The old man says to me, 'What did you dive off?' I says, 'To save my bloody life'. He says, 'What about me then?' (laughs) I nearly said, 'Every man for his bloody sen'.

ACTIVITY 7:

Select a member of the group who you think will read this story most effectively to the whole group. If you are working alone, record yourself reading the story. When you listen to the story, do *not* read it off the page, just use your aural skills and imagination.

ACTIVITY 8:

Before reading any further, discuss what rhetorical devices Jack Hill uses in the telling of this story. Write up your notes into a short report. Then compare your answer with the analysis below.

On first hearing, this story might seem a funny, exaggerated anecdote about a strange accident. But if we examine the story more closely, we can see a careful rhetorical strategy in Jack Hill's telling. For example, after the ritual entry into the story world ('That were another good time'), we go not to the obvious comic centre of the story – the narrative of the horse and piano – but to a seemingly inconsequential dialogue between Jack and his dad. The accident with the piano is skilfully managed with its increase in pace at the moment that the horse is lifted and in its management of potentially distracting information (for example, Jack Hill holds back the information that his father was 'a cripple' to the last possible moment, and the seriousness of his father's predicament – 'it could have killed him' – is only made clear *after* we've laughed). But what suggests the real rhetorical skill of the telling is the final section in which we find a mirror image of that 'irrelevant' opening dialogue. At the beginning the father made a peremptory demand that Jack go piano-shifting after a day in the pit. Jack saw the implications of the demand (the eloquent 'Ew'), agreed, but asserted his rights to his tea. At the end Jack's father is faced with the consequences of his own shoddy work ('I don't know whether he were drunk or what') but still makes unreasonable demands of his son – 'What did you dive off for?', 'What about me then?' This time Jack has the last word with a good punchline – 'Every man for his bloody sen'. Except that he doesn't. In the narrative he says nothing, leaving it to Jack the narrator to fill in the silence. And that's because the story is more about fathers and sons than horses and pianos. The 'real' story is in the frame, and the skilful shaping of the narrative allows the tensions and respects of that relationship to be explored while we laugh at the slapstick of a suspended horse.

Jack Hill's sophisticated story was told, not written. He had shaped its narrative, organised its information and dramatised its performance for the effects that he wanted, and, as we've seen, those effects are quite complicated ones. Jack Hill was an excellent story-teller – many of his stories are equally as thoughtful as this – and some people seem to have the gift for such performances. But, like any other rhetorical act, techniques of organisation, discourse and performance can be learned. The American writer Mark Twain, author of *Huckleberry Finn*, was also an accomplished stage story-teller, and in his essay 'How to Tell a Story' (1895) he suggests some of the methods to use when telling a comic story. It should be 'told gravely' he insists, without any explanations or overmuch emphasis. It should be apparently loosely organised, almost improvised, with important points dropped in casually (remember Jack Hill's brief comment on the horse's weight), and the story must be told patiently, with careful attention to silences and pauses (Twain 1996: 4–5).

ACTIVITY 9:

Twain provides a comic ghost story as an example and encourages his reader to practise telling it. Try performing this version of Twain's story, experimenting with your voice to achieve different effects, trying out different pace, volume and tones until you achieve the effect that you want. Twain claimed that if he did it properly he could always make someone in the audience shriek at the end. 'Mind you look out for the pause', he writes, 'and get it right'.

Once upon a time there was a really mean man and he lived way out in the prairie all alone with his wife. One day she died, and he carried her way out into the prairie and buried her. Well, she had a golden arm – all solid gold, from the shoulder down. He was really mean – really mean. And that night he couldn't sleep because he wanted that golden arm so much. When it got to midnight he couldn't stand it any more, so he gets up and takes his lantern and went out through the storm and dug her up and got the golden arm. And he bent his head down against the wind and he ploughed and ploughed and ploughed through the snow. Then all of a sudden he stops [*make a considerable pause here and look startled, and take a listening attitude*] and says: 'Lord, what's that?'

And he listens and he listens and the wind says [*set your teeth together and imitate the wailing and wheezing singsong of the wind*] 'Szzzz-z-zzz'. And then way back from where the grave is he hears a *voice*. He hears a voice all mixed up in the wind – he could hardly tell them apart – 'Szzz-zzz W-h-o-'s-g-o-t-m-y-g-o-l-d-e-n-*a-r-m*?' [*you must begin to shiver violently now*].

And he began to shiver and shake and say, 'Oh my Lord, oh my Lord,' and the wind blows the lantern out, and the snow and the sleet blows in his face and almost chokes him, and he starts ploughing knee-deep towards home, almost dead he's so scared. And soon he hears the voice again and [*pause*] it's coming *after* him. 'Szzzz-zzz W-h-o-'s-g-o-t-m-y-g-o-l-d-e-n-*a-r-m*?'

When he gets to the pasture he hears it again – closer now and *coming*! coming back in the dark and in the storm [*repeat the wind and the voice*]. When he gets to the house he rushes upstairs and jumps in the bed and covers up his head and ears and lies shivering and shaking. And then way out there he hears it *again* – coming! And soon he hears [*pause – awed, silent listening attitude*] – pat-pat-pat – *it's coming upstairs*. Then he hears the latch and he knows it's in the room.

Soon he knows it's *standing by the bed*. Then he knows it's *bending down over him* – and he can barely get his breath. Then – then he feels something *c-o-l-d* right down almost against his head.

Then the voice says *right at his ear* 'W-h-o-'s-g-o-t-m-y-g-o-l-d-e-n-a-r-m?' [*You must wail it out very plaintively and accusingly; then you stare steadily and impassively into the face of one of the audience and let that awe-inspiring pause begin to build itself in the deep hush. When it has reached exactly the right length, jump up suddenly at that person and yell*] 'You've got it!'

(adapted from Twain 1996: 10–12)

ACTIVITY 10:

Think of a good story-teller that you know – it doesn't matter what kind of stories, just someone that you like to listen to. Write down everything that you can think of as to why s/he is good: what kinds of stories, how are they organised, what kind of language, where are they told, how long do they last, what does s/he do with her/his body, what kind of audiences are there, how are the audiences acknowledged? Try to record/write down one of the stories. Bring it to the class, and explain to your group how the story works.

Mark Twain 'borrowed' the golden arm story from African-American tradition, adapting it to his own voice, and I have similarly adapted Twain's voice for English speakers. That's because, unless people are particularly good mimics or trained in voice skills, it is much easier to be rhetorically effective in your normal speech patterns. Nevertheless, we can learn a lot from the rhetorical practices of different cultures which, as well as being enjoyable, point up the features of the cultures that we work in and may not notice because they seem 'natural'. African-American sermons, for example, are far more rhetorically emphatic than those of contemporary English traditions.

The African-derived verbal contests termed signifying, ranking or dissin' (the ritual exchange of insults) or the concept of 'lying' (telling extravagant stories that the audience accepts as extravagant) are rhetorical performances that are far less common in white cultures. The black-American comedian Richard Pryor used to exploit white misunderstanding of these rhetorical conventions by having a white supervisor reply to a ritual insult, 'we can surely communicate on a higher plane than *that*' (for an excellent discussion of African-American rhetorical forms see Watkins 1994).

The Jamaican poet and story-teller Louise Bennett also uses the language and rhetorical performance style of an African-derived culture in her work – work that established Jamaican as a language for poetry, drama and performance. The extract that follows is from one of her Radio Jamaica broadcasts in which she plays the part of Miss Lou, a forceful Jamaican woman who puts forward the views of her even more forceful Aunty Roachy. In this performance the subject is the population explosion in Jamaica. The extract demonstrates the power of the particular speech rhythms of a culture, and introduces Aunty Roachy's rhetorical skills in her public 'cussin out' of the irresponsible father Tata One-stump:

My Aunty Roachy seh dat it sweet her to see dat mose a de smaddy-dem weh dah shake dem fis eena population explosion face belongs to de opposite (male) sex!

An it sweet her becausen seh dat when youh hear some certain man folks talk you woulda never know seh dat de male sex got anyting fi to do wid population explosion! Heh-heh! Everybody attackin de explosion an nobody naw attack all de exploders-dem! Mmmm.

Some people dah meck joke seh dat all over Jamaica all yuh can hear is *boom, boom, boom, boom, boom, boom,* 'Mamma, mamma, mamma, mamma, mamma, mamma!' An Aunty Roachy seh she woulda like fi know what happen to 'Papa, papa, pap!' An as she seh de wud so, she look hard pon Tata One-stump.

Hear Tata, 'What a good ting dat jamaica wasn a suffer from population explosion bout tirty years agao! For me discover jus las week seh dat me got a married daughter dat study over Englan, an me hope she will adop me in me ole age.'

See yah! Aunty Roachy call down Tata One-stump, yuh see, an she tell him seh, 'Tata, yuh shoulda heng dung yuh head wid shame anytime yuh member dat daughter, for yuh never ac like no fahder to dat poor gal from de day she born! Yuh never know how she eat, drink, or wear clothes, an if wasn fi de gal mumma side a de family help an ambition she woulda tun eena ragamuffin an a box bout pon street, an she woulda did dead from hungry an malnutrition long time, an yuh wouldn have no daughter fi boas bout an a beg fi adop yuh eena yuh ole age!'

Tata gi out, 'Hmmn, a true. Me never did look afah dah gal. But look omuch gal pickney puppa dead lef dem from dem bawn! Sposen me did dead?'

Aunty Roachy seh, 'But yuh never dead! Yuh is a big trong an hearty man a shirk yuh responsibility as fahder! An now yuh a come boas bout daughter over Englan when yuh didn even treat her as no daughter in Jamaica!'

Heh-hey! Tata One-stump shut up him mout, *pam.*

Aunty Roachy holler, 'Yuh ole population exploder yuh!'

Ay ya yie!

(Bennett 1993: 73–5)

ACTIVITY 11:

Try reading Louise Bennett's story out loud. The Jamaican spelling system, by which 'non-standard' English is translated from speech to page, forces us to learn the rhythms of another rhetoric (unless, of course, you already speak Jamaican!). What different sounds, emphasis, volume and styles do you need to use to make the story effective?

ACTIVITY 12:

In groups, take turns to tell a story, experience, or joke. The main aim here is to capture the attention of your audience through some of the devices explored in this chapter. Do *not* write down your story. If you think you will forget something, make minimal notes, just to prompt your memory. When everyone has had a chance to tell a 'story', discuss which ones were most effective and why. If you are working on your own, try recording yourself telling the story and then playing it back to analyse your success.

In this chapter we have suggested that rhetoric is a means of performance and persuasion that is part of everyday life. 'Classical' rhetoric still influences important areas of public discourse, but it is just one part of a range of devices for putting across a point. Whether we are listening to a good story, watching an advertisement or trying to write a speech for a wedding, we are part of a living rhetorical world.

Summary

In this chapter we have been exploring the use of rhetoric in contemporary cultures including:

- rhetoric in the courtroom
- rhetoric in selling
- story-telling
- the rhetorical conventions of formal speeches.

References

Atkinson, Rowan (1995) *Rowan Atkinson*. LaffC46 (audio-cassette).

Benjamin, Walter (1973) *Illuminations*, trans. H. Zohn. London: Fontana/Collins.

Bennett, Louise (1993) *Aunty Roachy Seh*, ed. M. Morris. Kingston, Jamaica: Sangster's Bookstores.

Brierley, Sean (1995) *The Advertising Handbook*. London: Routledge.

Clark, Colin and Pinch, Trevor (1995) *The Hard Sell*. London: HarperCollins.

Cook, Guy (1992) *The Discourse of Advertising*. London: Routledge.

Ellis, Patrick (1992) *Who Dares Sells*. London: Thorssons.

Gibbons, John (ed.) (1994) *Language and the Law*. London and New York: Longman.

Hopkins, Tom (1994) *How to Master the Art of Selling*. London: HarperCollins.

Howe, David (1993) *On Being a Client: Understanding the Process of Counselling and Psychotherapy*. London: Sage Publications.

Lansbury, Angela (1988) *Wedding Speeches and Toasts*. London: Ward Lock.

Mamet, David (1984) *Glengarry Glen Ross*. London: Methuen.

Nevett, T.R. (1982) *Advertising in Britain: A History*. London: Heinemann.

Ong, Walter (1982) *Orality and Literacy: The Technologizing of the Word*. London: Methuen.

Pottle, Pat (1991) 'Members of the Jury . . .', *The Guardian*, 27 June 1991.

Turner, E.S. (1952) *The Shocking History of Advertising*. London: Michael Joseph.

Twain, Mark (1996) *How to Tell a Story and Other Essays*. New York and Oxford: Oxford University Press.

Twelftree, Graham (1996) *Getting the Point Across: 200 Effective and Entertaining Stories for Speakers, Preachers and Teachers*. Cape Town: SCB Publishers / Crowborough: Monarch.

Watkins, Mel (1994) *On the Real Side: Laughing, Lying and Signifying*. New York: Touchstone.

CHAPTER 5

Preparing your case

Rebecca Stott

I n this chapter we will be looking at the skills needed for preparing a short presentation and in the following chapter we will then go on to look at presentation skills themselves. Across these two very practical chapters we will be concentrating on the processes of preparing and delivering a spoken argument, not as a formal speech given to hundreds or thousands of people, but rather a short presentation to a small group of people in a seminar or workplace.

When is a presentation helpful?

Well-planned and delivered presentations can be a very effective way of informing, persuading or instructing. People tend to use the term presentation to describe more informal kinds of public speaking. Unlike formal large-scale lectures and public speeches, for instance, in which interaction between speaker and audience is very much limited by the size of the audience, presentations tend to be used to present ideas and information in an (at least potentially) interactive way. They can be a particularly effective way to put across concepts and complex ideas because the presenter can use overhead projector transparencies and other visual aids and because the audience can ask for further clarification as and when they need it. Presentation can be effective as a means of persuading because the presenter can engage directly with counter-arguments in discussion with the audience as such issues occur. They can also be entertaining and this sometimes helps facilitate discussion and understanding.

However, presentations are not always the best way of communicating and you should make sure that what you want to communicate is suitable for a presentation before you begin. Practical subjects, for instance, cannot be taught well using only the presentation method as people can usually only develop practical skills by actually practising them. However, a presentation might be useful as a way of presenting the theory behind the practice. A skydiving tutor, for instance, might begin a series of lessons with a presentation with slides and overhead transparencies on the structure of the parachute. Factual material can be presented very well using the presentation method, but if the presentation contains nothing else (no reflection, analysis or judgement, for instance) it is probably better given in another form – a report for instance, which could be circulated before a meeting or seminar. Then in the meeting it might be useful for someone to give a presentation about the implications and likely repercussions of the information in the report, for instance, which would serve as the starting point for discussion.

Before we turn to discussing techniques for preparing a presentation, we would like you to reflect upon your current speaking and presentation skills in order to help you define the areas in which you need practice and advice.

ACTIVITY 1:

Imagine you are a recruitment and training consultant and you are interviewing a new client who is looking for work in which the ability to give short presentations to small groups will be very important (there are so many jobs that require these skills: for example, company representatives, teachers, marketing consultants, equal opportunity or careers advisers, legal advocates, social workers). In pairs take it in turn to interview the other person about his or her current speaking abilities and past experience. You should take notes and work towards the identification of key areas that need improvement. You might want to use some or all of the following questions:

- What experience of formal presentations have you had before – in education or elsewhere (chairing a discussion, giving a formal presentation to an audience, giving informal presentations to a peer group, participating in debate, for instance)?
- Have you had any instruction in these areas, such as training in 'public speaking' or presentations at school, or training in business presentations at work? How useful did you find this training?
- Have you had any experience in communicating complicated or technical information to a non-specialist audience? How well did you do?
- If you were required to give a formal five-minute presentation which required a level of research and was delivered to a group of five to ten people, what would you need to improve in terms of your skills at present? What can you already do well?

Preparation: knowing your audience

You do not need to be trained in formal rhetoric to know that the work that goes on behind the scenes in preparing for a presentation is just as important as the presentation itself. A presentation may be beautifully delivered with great eloquence and style, but if the argument has not been thought through clearly, if it has not been tailored to the particular audience, if the evidence is weak, it is unlikely to be persuasive. We have been arguing in this book that one of the most important ways of measuring the success of an argument is whether it persuades the audience to whom it is addressed. Effective arguments need to be researched, defined and structured before they can be delivered.

As we have already pointed out, arguments must not only be shaped, defined and structured, but they must also be put together with a particular audience in mind. A recently produced business training video about presentation skills, presented and acted by Dawn French, presents a story about a senior administrator asked to give a presentation to senior managers about the advantages of a relocation of the site of their organisation (BBC 1997). Let's call her Sarah. Sarah, nervous about the task ahead of her, nonetheless does a very good job. She spends time researching her subject. She talks to the people behind the relocation plans and asks them to explain to her what they see as the advantages of moving. She finds out what the senior managers think about the new site and what their concerns are. She finds pictures and plans and information about the new site and transfers these into high-quality slides and overhead transparencies. As she structures her talk she addresses specific concerns expressed by the senior managers in her early discussions with them. She tells them about the advantages of moving both for the organisation and for them as individuals: better car-parking facilities for senior managers, health clubs in the area, good relocation packages. She gives her presentation. She persuades her audience. The presentation is a success.

A few weeks later her boss, delighted by the quality of her presentation, asks her to give another presentation about relocation, this time to the administrators and support staff of the organisation. Knowing that she has put in a great deal of time and energy and that she has excellent visual aids, she decides, without much thought, to give the *same* presentation. You will probably be able to anticipate the outcome. The first presentation had been designed and prepared for a very different audience. For the first presentation she put her mind to persuading senior managers. However, the arguments for persuading this new group are simply not the same because their concerns and the impact of relocation on their working lives will inevitably be different. Because she hasn't spent time talking to members of this new audience, the presenter does not know what their concerns are. Nor has she found out what the relocation packages will be for this group. The presentation, the overhead transparencies, the information presented are not a success. In fact the presentation has probably worked to alienate the second audience. By concentrating on all the advantages that the senior managers will gain from the relocation, she has presented the relocation as though it has only been planned with senior managers in mind.

This example, of course, illustrates our very simple but critical point: you must have your audience specifically in mind when you are preparing your material whatever the nature of your presentation, whether you are working for a business, presenting a conference paper on Heidegger, or explaining current debates in literary theory to your peers in a seminar.

ACTIVITY 2:

Sometimes when presenters need to explain complex information to their audience they find it difficult to put themselves in the shoes of a member of their audience and to imagine what that person's needs might be in terms of being able to understand the information given. This activity is designed to illustrate the importance of being able to see yourself through your audience's eyes and to be able to judge the effectiveness of the information you give in terms of their needs. On a piece of A4 paper one member of your group should draw a complex abstract diagram using triangles, circles, squares or rectangles connected by lines such as the one we have assembled below. It should fill the paper space.

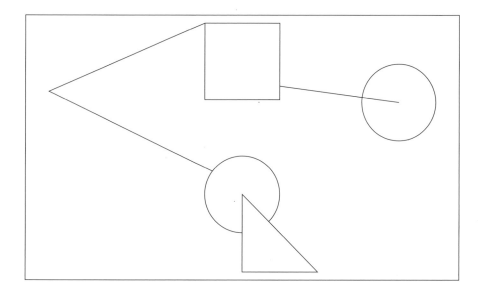

The rest of the group should not see the diagram. This member of the group should now take five or ten minutes to try to describe the diagram clearly enough so that the other members of the group can draw it on their own pieces of paper. At the end of the time, the group members should compare their drawing with the original. Now discuss the task. What did the presenter do or not do to make the description clearer? What could s/he have done differently? What did the audience need the presenter to do? Write up your notes into a short report.

ACTIVITY 3:

The following activity needs no research and it should be possible to complete simply by jotting down key points. Think of a subject about which you feel strongly – so strongly that you would be prepared to speak about it in front of others in order to persuade them of your position. Now write down a list of between six and ten people whom you know (not necessarily well) who would not share your views but who nonetheless would be prepared to listen to your views with an open mind. Next to their names write down a few sentences or keywords about what their individual positions are likely to be on this subject. Now, with this specific audience in mind, write down five reasons why you think this group should change their minds about the issue or subject. Transfer these reasons into keywords. If you are working in a group, address the other group members as if they were your assumed audience. You have only three minutes to present your view.

ACTIVITY 4:

Most university libraries stock an annual publication called *The Year's Work in English Studies* (Blackwell) which provides a yearly listing of articles and books of literary criticism in the following categories: English language, Old English literature, Middle English, Chaucer, Sixteenth Century, Shakespeare, and Renaissance Drama; it also lists them by critic, author and subject area.

Choose one of the following authors: Charles Dickens, George Eliot, James Joyce or Virginia Woolf. Then choose a year between 1985 and 1992. Now visit the library and find the volume of *The Year's Work in English* for your chosen year and photocopy the entry. Alternatively, you could use the extract from the entry on Postcolonialism for 1995 below.

> Judie Newman's *The Ballistic Bard: Postcolonial Fictions* examines a varied selection of contemporary texts by African, Indian and Caribbean writers in relation to issues of intertextuality. The starting point is 'the relation between postcolonial literature and its predecessors', as suggested by the title's reference to J.G. Farrell's *The Siege of Krishnapur*, where connections are made between British military and cultural domination of India in the nineteenth century. Newman makes interesting use of the contrasting ways in which Anita Desai and Ruth Prawer Jhabvala appropriate and rewrite Forster's *A Passage to India*, in *Baumgartner's Bombay* and *Heat and Dust*. The practice of reading 'new' literatures in relation to canonical texts to

highlight their simultaneous imbrication with and resistance to metropolitan discourses has produced some fruitful discussion in recent years, and this study makes a valuable contribution to that project, but it is also concerned with a far wider range of reference, allowing Newman to argue that these texts are far from simply dependent on the centre, and doomed to rework the canon.

...*Indian-English Fiction 1980–1990: An Assessment* (1994) is a collection of 18 essays originally given as papers at a University of Bombay seminar in 1991. The editors, Nilufer E. Bharucha and Vilas Sarang, suggest that the 1980s saw Indian fiction in English 'liberated from the colonial yoke' and becoming 'an integral part of the Indian environment', with a substantial indigenous readership and a legitimate role in Indian literature.... The bulk of the volume is, however, devoted to interesting detailed analysis of specific writers, themes and groupings. The range is impressively wide, and the individual contributions maintain a high standard. Work published by older writers during the decade is considered alongside the work of the many new novelists to emerge, with single author studies of Salman Rushdie, Shashi Deshpande, Rohinton Mistry, Bharati Mukherjee, Amitav Ghosh, Nayantara Sahgal, Anita Desai, Raja Rao and R.K. Narayan. The importance of women writers is stressed, as is the major contribution made by novelists from the Parsi community. There are also pieces that address the specific concerns of the many expatriate writers that are claimed by the field, and some useful essays on the urban experience, autobiographical aspects and novels of the Partition.

(Kitson 1998: 765–6)

Your aim is to prepare a short presentation for the members of your group that *summarises* the critical work undertaken on your chosen author or subject in that particular year. You have a maximum of five minutes to present your summary and assessment and you should do so with no notes, although you are permitted to write down names of critics and authors, if you need to do so (as a reminder).

Think about your audience – what do they know and what do you need to explain to them? How can you make your summary and assessment interesting, useful and relevant to your audience? If you were in that audience what kind of presentation would you find useful, interesting and relevant? Finally, remember that your presentation should do more than simply summarise the information. Make sure that your presentation, by processing, shaping, framing and contextualising the information, serves a particular function which is to aid discussion in a seminar dedicated to exploring contemporary critical reactions to your particular author or subject.

ACTIVITY 5:

Below is an extract from a nineteenth-century text called *The Idea of a University* (1852), in which the author, Cardinal Newman, defines his views on the role of a university and of a liberal education. These written arguments were actually part of a series of lectures given to the newly founded Catholic University of Ireland, in which John Henry Newman was rector for a few years. Newman was writing at a time when many important legislators were arguing that a useful education 'should be confined to some particular and narrow end, and should issue in some definite work, which can be weighed and measured' (Newman 1986: 1016). Newman is therefore arguing against this position.

You are working as a parliamentary researcher and the MP you work for is drafting a presentation to be given to a small but very powerful sub-committee of politicians looking at the future of higher education. The MP knows that a large number of members of this committee feel very strongly that higher education should become more vocational. She disagrees and is trying to put together a set of arguments proposing that a broad liberal arts education is valuable for its own sake. She knows that Cardinal Newman made a series of arguments about this in the nineteenth century and has asked you to find out about the key points of his argument so that she might refer to the passage in questions after her presentation. You have found this passage but you only have time to read it through a couple of times and perhaps make the sketchiest of notes. Because she is also short on time, she has asked you to brief her as she walks between her office and the committee meeting room, a walk that takes about three minutes. You have only fifteen minutes to prepare your briefing, which includes reading time. What will you say? Give your briefing orally and without notes as if you were actually in the situation described.

I have been insisting, in my two preceding Discourses, first, on the cultivation of the intellect, as an end which may reasonably be pursued for its own sake; and next, on the nature of that cultivation, or what that cultivation consists in. Truth of whatever kind is the proper object of the intellect; its cultivation then lies in fitting it to apprehend and contemplate truth. Now the intellect in its present state, with exceptions which need not here be specified, does not discern truth intuitively, or as a whole. We know, not by a direct and simple vision, not at a glance, but, as it were, by piecemeal and accumulation, by a mental process, by going round an object, by the comparison, the combination, the mutual correction, the continual adaptation, of many partial notions, by the employment, concentration, and joint action of many faculties and exercises of mind. Such a union and concert of the intellectual powers, such an enlargement and development, such a comprehensiveness, is necessarily a matter of training. And again, such a training is a matter of rule; it is not mere application, however exemplary, which introduces the mind to truth, nor the reading many books, nor the getting up many subjects, nor the witnessing many experiments, nor the attending many lectures. All this is short of enough; a man may have done it all, yet be lingering in the vestibule of knowledge: he may not realise what his mouth utters; he may not see with his mental eye what confronts him; he may have no grasp of things as they are; or at least he may have no power at all of advancing one step forward of himself, in consequence of what he has already acquired, no power of discriminating between truth and falsehood, of sifting out the truth from the mass, of arranging things according to their real value, and, if I may use the phrase, of building up ideas. Such a power is the result of a scientific formation of mind; it is an acquired faculty of judgement, of clearsightedness, of sagacity, of wisdom, of philosophical reach of mind, and of intellectual self-possession and repose – qualities which do not come of mere acquirement. The bodily eye, the organ for apprehending material objects, is provided by nature; the eye of the mind, of which the object is truth, is the work of discipline and habit.

This process of training, by which the intellect, instead of being formed or sacrificed to some particular or accidental purpose, some specific trade or profession, or study or science, is disciplined for its own sake, for the perception of its own proper object, and for its own highest culture, is called Liberal Education; and though there is no one in whom it is carried as far as is conceivable, or whose intellect would be a pattern of what intellects should be made, yet there is scarcely anyone but may gain an idea of what real training is, and at least look towards it, and make its true scope and result, not something else, his standard of excellence; and numbers there are who may submit themselves to it, and secure it to themselves in good measure. And to set forth the right standard, and to train according to it, and to help forward all students toward it according to their various capacities, this I conceive to be the business of a University.

(Newman 1986: 1015–6)

Here are some other specific scenarios, all very different, in which an argument (or a cluster of arguments) needs to be made to a particular audience in a particular place and time.

Scenario 1

You are a student in a seminar group studying contemporary poetry and your tutor has asked you to introduce this poem by James Berry to the rest of the seminar group. You have two objectives: to offer a reading of the poem in the light of Stewart Brown's characterisation of Berry's poetry as 'celebration with an echo of despair'; and to argue that knowledge of Berry and his Jamaican upbringing are important contexts for a fuller understanding of this poem. You have ten minutes to present the poem and to make this argument. Your seminar group have not read any poetry by James Berry before and you believe that they probably have read very little contemporary Jamaican poetry. Here is the entry on Berry in the anthology from which this is taken, *The POW Anthology* (Horowitz and Laird 1996):

James Berry

Growing up in Jamaica, Berry felt as much disturbed by his African background as by the European slave-trade and its aftermath. His scintillating anthology *News for Babylon* (Chatto and Windus 1984) brought the new dawn of Anglo-Caribbean bards home to the mainstream readership, and his latest volume, *Hot Earth Cold Earth* (Bloodaxe 1995), shows him writing at the height of his powers at the age of 70. (Horowitz and Laird 1996: 80)

'On an Afternoon Train from Purley to Victoria, 1955' by James Berry

Hello, she said and startled me.
Nice day. Nice day I agreed.
I am a Quaker she said and Sunday

I was moved in silence
to speak a poem loudly
for racial brotherhood.

I was thoughtful, then said
what poem came on like that?
One the moment inspired she said.
I was again thoughtful.

Inexplicably I saw
empty city streets lit dimly
in a day's first hours.
Alongside in darkness
was my father's big banana field.

Where are you from? she said
Jamaica I said.
What part of Africa is Jamaica? she said.
Where Ireland is near Lapland I said.
Hard to see why you leave
such sunny country she said.
Snow falls elsewhere I said.
So sincere she was beautiful
as people sat down around us.
(Berry 1985)

Scenario 2

You are the first-year student representative on the English Department Board. The department is currently assessing the first-year courses (or modules) of its English degree programme in order to identify where the first-year programme needs to be changed to meet the needs and interests of first-year students. You have been asked to consult as widely as possible with first-year students and to come up with a series of recommendations for change. Your task is not only to present such recommendations to the Board (made up of all the teaching staff in your department) but also to argue for why they are necessary. You have been allocated a ten-minute slot on the agenda and will be expected to answer questions.

Scenario 3

The Student Union (SU) is opposed to a government proposal of an increase in the student contribution to fees. You have been elected to act as an SU spokesperson to persuade the local business community to write to their MPs protesting against increases in student fees. You have been invited to the annual regional gathering of the Chamber of Commerce (which is usually attended by over 100 members) and have been allocated a slot of ten minutes in which to make your case to this audience. You may wish to draw on some of Newman's ideas (see passage from *The Idea of a University*) or to consult the Dearing Report available on-line (http://www.leeds.ac.uk/educol/ncihe/) in order to help establish your case about the value of higher education to the wider community and the need for greater government subsidy of students. Ten minutes have been allocated to questions and discussion afterwards.

Scenario 4

You work for a large computer company based in the centre of Cambridge. You are one of the senior managers responsible for, amongst other things, managing the site (and car park) on which the business is built. You have decided that your company should take a leading role in reducing the traffic congestion in the centre of the city by encouraging your employees to use bicycles to travel to work rather than bringing in their cars. You have placed an item on the agenda of the next meeting of the Senior Management Committee (six to eight members). You expect that many of the members of this committee will oppose the issue because they are all car users themselves. There are many items on the agenda so time is at a premium. You have ten minutes to make your case to the committee and suggest some ways in which the number of staff travelling to work by car might be reduced and the reasons for such changes. After that the chair of the meeting has allotted half an hour of discussion time.

In Chapter 2 we explained that one of the most famous Roman rhetoricians, Quintillian (writing in AD 94), broke down the process of constructing a piece of rhetoric or argument into three stages:

- invention: the finding of arguments or proofs
- disposition: the arrangement of such matters
- style: the choice of words, verbal patterns and rhythms that will most effectively express the material.

For the purposes of this chapter we will follow Quintillian's stages one by one and will use the four scenarios above to focus on the different stages.

Invention or gathering material

This is perhaps the most vital and creative stage in the process that will lead to the delivery of a piece of argumentation. A more contemporary term for it might be 'brainstorming'. This involves careful attention to the case that you are making, to the needs and characteristics of the specific audience, and to the evidence needed to persuade this particular audience.

The scenarios above appear to be very different but they have things in common. They all specify an audience. They are all time-limited. They will all require some research and will need to be tightly organised if the audience is to be persuaded within the time allowed. As the presentations will form the basis of subsequent discussion, the presenters will need to anticipate the kinds of concerns, interests, prejudices and questions that will arise in the discussion from this particular audience.

Excavating the context

Any presenter needs to know and understand the wider picture of the case s/he is arguing. Sometimes this will involve reading; sometimes it will involve talking to people. In Scenario 2 (changes to the first-year English programme), for instance, a series of discussions with both staff and students will be essential to gather opinions and points of view, whereas Scenario 1 (the poem) will need more library research. You might want to ask informed people where they would start if this was their task. Who should I speak to? What should I read? Why is this important? What do I need to know?

ACTIVITY 6:

Choose one of the scenarios above and state how you will go about excavating the wider context. Who might you approach in order to discuss the task? What books might you consult? What other resources might be helpful?

Identifying your objective

Identifying your objective early on will save a lot of time later. It will also help you to focus clearly as you gather and structure your material and judge the success of your final presentation. The objective of Scenario 1 for instance has two parts: to offer a reading of the poem in the light of Stewart Brown's characterisation of Berry's poetry as 'celebration with an echo of despair'; and to argue that knowledge of Berry and his Jamaican upbringing are important contexts for a fuller understanding of this poem. The objective of Scenario 3 is more directly persuasive: to persuade your audience to write to their MPs about student fees. The objective of Scenario 4 (car-parking strategies) is more practical and focused on providing recommendations for action.

Thinking about your audience

We argued earlier that every presentation needs to be geared to a particular audience and the more you know about that audience the better.

ACTIVITY 7:

Using the same scenario you chose earlier, write down a series of notes about the audience you will be addressing. What do your audience already know and what do they need to know? What objections might your audience have to the position you will be arguing? What are the counter-arguments and how might you address them? How can you make sure that you keep the audience interested and involved?

Thinking round the issues

Depending on the nature of your task there will be a series of issues at stake. Sometimes your task will be to argue one main point, but sometimes there will be several key points that need to be argued. In order to argue the case well you will need to think around the issues and be able to see them from many different vantage points. The nineteenth-century writer John Ruskin once wisely said:

> Mostly matters of any consequence are three-sided, or four-sided, or polygonal, and the trotting round a polygon is severe work for people in any way stiff in their opinions.

> (Ruskin 1903–12: 16.184)

You are generally more likely to get agreement from your audience if you are able to present a well-rounded view of your subject. Otherwise your audience may feel that they have only been given a partial view and will feel it their duty to draw your attention to all the other possible sides to the issue. It will be useful to be able to anticipate other people's views on the matter, even if, finally, your job is to persuade the audience of one particular point of view.

ACTIVITY 8:

Still working with the scenario you selected earlier, jot down as many different ideas as you can about this particular issue. You might want to write them in the form of a list or perhaps use a spider-diagram. Gather evidence to support each of the main points and try to anticipate what arguments might be used against them. The final result is likely to be a mixture of bits of information, research information, points of view, evidence, arguments and counter-arguments.

At this point you will probably be able to see that you have produced more information and evidence and points of view than you can cover in the allotted time and that your material badly needs organisation. Brainstorming will usually result in an overproduction of material so you will need to do some careful editing. This brings us to the next stage of the preparation: disposition or arrangement.

Disposition or arrangement of material

Now is the time to return to your objective and to try to decide how you can meet it in the time allotted. You might want to consider identifying three to five main points perhaps. Be careful with your choices here and jettison anything that is not going to help you achieve your objective. Be careful not to put too much in. Some people have a tendency to treat arguments as hold-alls into which they stuff as much as possible. When this happens the presentation will be weighed down with too much detail and it will be difficult for the audience to work out what you consider the key points to be.

In deciding what evidence to choose you should be guided by your objective and by your audience. What do they already know and what do they need you to tell them? What will persuade them? What might be their objections? All of these questions will help you to find a shape for your presentation.

ACTIVITY 9:

Put together a skeleton plan of between three and five main points or sections for your talk, showing how each of your main points will contribute to your final objective. Take a look at your plan and ask yourself whether you can cover all this material in the time allowed. Redraft it to ensure that you can meet your objective in the time. You will need to ask yourself:

- What is your objective?
- What are 'the means of persuasion' in this case?
- What is relevant/not relevant?
- What are the most important points and will they persuade this audience?
- What evidence is most effective and persuasive and what does this evidence prove in terms of your selected main points?
- How will you arrange the material so that it is most effective with your audience?
- How will you show your audience that you have moved from one main point to another?
- How will you show the links or transitions between the different parts of the argument, the sequence of your argument and how each part connects to the others?

Transfer your plan to prompt cards with key points and information laid out clearly so that they will identify the order of the subject matter without you having to read anything word for word.

Style or expressing the argument

Quintillian identified style as the final key stage of the rhetorical process, and by this he meant the words used to express the ideas. As many speeches given to large crowds are in fact *written* by speech-writers, those writers can incorporate a number of rhetorical devices into the speech which will make it as effective as possible. If you look back at Blair's acceptance speech for instance, printed in Chapter 2, the language appears to be deliberately down-played and modest. It does not appear to be full of rhetorical flourishes but the speech-writer has indeed used word patterns and manipulation of syntax and parallel sentences in order to create an effect with the audience. This speech was written for delivery in front of a large audience and with an even larger audience in mind – the millions of listeners who would watch the speech on television or hear it on the radio.

Presentations of the kind outlined in the scenarios above are rather different. In all these cases the arguments are more likely to be successful if they can in some way be less like a monologue and more like a dialogue or conversation, with the speaker holding the floor for enough time to make a claim but anticipating that the claim will be open to question and discussion from the audience and the interlocutors. The context is much more intimate than a public speech. The effect will be much more like the give and take of a conversation. In all these scenarios if you were to give a formal written speech like that of Tony Blair or Hillary Clinton you'd probably end up with a hostile audience or you'd be laughed out of the room because the register would be wrong and the audience would feel that you were talking not to them but to another imagined audience of hundreds, assembled perhaps outside the windows of the seminar room.

So using the style of the formal speech would not do here. But how do you find a way of expressing your material that will work with this audience of your peers (Scenario 1) or lecturers (Scenario 2) or unknown business people (Scenario 3) or work colleagues (Scenario 4)? If you write out every word it will sound stilted and inflexible; it will be obvious that it is a written piece and may alienate your audience. However, if you don't write down anything you will run the risk of forgetting your material. How do you remember all your material, make things clear, relevant and interesting, and make sure that your audience are interested enough to want to ask questions at the end?

Some presenters think in terms of telling a story when they structure their presentations. Someone giving a presentation on the impact of Marxist theory on literary criticism, for instance, might start by giving the contextual and introductory material as if it were the beginning of a story, telling the audience about the emergence of Marxist criticism in the post-war years and why it mattered to people. Then they might tell the audience about the shape of Marxist criticism at its peak in the 1970s and 1980s and then go on to describe the way it changed with the impact of new ideas about the workings of power in the 1990s.

ACTIVITY 10:

Think about a presentation you have heard recently that you thought was particularly good. Identify what it was about this presentation and the presenter that made it successful. Did the presenter use handouts or overhead projectors or a white board for key points? How was the material presented? Did you have a clear sense of structure or stages of an argument? How was the structure made clear to you? How much information were you given? How did the presenter keep your attention and keep you engaged? Then think about how you can use some of this successful practice to build into your own presentation. You might want to consider the following questions:

- How can you express this argument most compellingly and interestingly?
- How will you ensure that you put across your arguments effectively and at the same time remember everything (notes, prompt cards etc.)?
- What will your audience need to ensure that they remember the most important points and can engage fully in discussion after you have finished speaking?
- Are you going to use visual aids in any way (handouts, material on the board, overhead projector)?
- How can you use narrative in your argument, if at all?
- Where can you use anecdotes, analogies and examples?
- Where will you need to go very slowly – if the material is difficult or dense for example?
- How can you use your first few minutes most effectively?
- How can you use your last few minutes most effectively?

Write up your answers as a short report.

ACTIVITY 11:

Look back over the material you have drawn up. How effective will this presentation be, do you think? Imagine you had several more days to refine it. What would you want to do to make it more effective? Where are the weakest points in the argument and how might you strengthen these?

ACTIVITY 12:

Reflect on the preparation process you have just been through. What do you find most straightforward, and what do you find more difficult in the process? What are your strengths and weaknesses in formulating an argument of this kind? Write up a short report reflecting on the process and your own participation in it. You might want to reflect on other occasions where you have been asked to give a presentation or to argue a particular point of view. What have you done well in the past? Check back over your answers to the interview earlier in this chapter and report on what specific improvements you have made thus far.

Summary

In this chapter we have explored:

- the nature and usefulness of presentations
- the importance of knowing your audience
- the importance of knowing your objective
- techniques for brainstorming and gathering material
- techniques for ordering and prioritising material.

References

BBC (1997) *Speak for Yourself: A Guide to Making Effective Presentations.* London: Acorn Press.

Berry, James (1985) *Chain of Days.* Oxford: Oxford University Press.

Horowitz, Michael and Laird, Inge Elsa (eds) (1996) *The POW Anthology.* London: New Departures.

Kitson, Peter J. (ed.) (1998) *The Year's Work in English Studies.* Oxford: Blackwell.

Newman, John Henry (1986) *The Idea of A University* [1852] in *Norton Anthology of English Literature* vol 2, 5th edition. W.W. Norton and Company.

Ruskin, John (1903–12) *The Works of John Ruskin*, ed. E.T. Cook and A. Wedderburn, 39 vols. London: George Allen.

Presenting your case

Cordelia Bryan

Few people are fortunate enough to be naturally accomplished public speakers. Most have had to learn some fundamental rules of good communication and practice in order to become effective in the art of oral presentation. Lloyd George, the famous orator and debater, was said to be like a cat on hot bricks before he had to speak in the House of Commons. He thoroughly prepared for his speeches with the help of Roget's Thesaurus and often wrote them out beforehand, then learned them by heart. All his preparation paid dividends. He was renowned as a brilliant phrase-maker who could sway his opponents with his eloquent and often witty rhetoric. He once described the House of Lords as simply '500 men chosen accidentally from the unemployed' (Grigg 1978: 156). To add to his skill with language he worked on dramatic talent and voice production to demand attention for the end-result of all his thorough preparation.

If the prospect of giving a presentation fills you with fear, you are in good company. In a famous survey of 3,000 American citizens, asked what they most feared 41 per cent placed public speaking top of their list, way above fear of sickness, loneliness or even of death (Wallechinsky, Wallace and Wallace 1977: 469). Reasons offered for this common dread of speaking in public vary, but all can be traced back to a fundamental human fear of making a fool of oneself in front of others. It is common sense to acknowledge that thorough preparation will minimise the risk of appearing foolish. Most of the best speeches, including those which appear spontaneous, are well stage-managed events prepared with a great deal of planning, rehearsing and hard work.

In this chapter we are assuming that you have prepared thoroughly (see previous chapter). Here we offer practical material intended to help you present your case as effectively as possible. We shall be focusing on some key guidelines for making your case in different contexts. By experimenting with bad practice you will remember, and so avoid in future, the worst and most commonly made errors in public speaking. We will show how constructive feedback from others can help to objectify a process which is all too often marred by fear and anxiety. Opportunities are provided for you to practise and develop both skills and confidence in giving effective oral presentations.

Public speaking is not so different from learning to play a musical instrument; the theory of music is of limited value unless you can actually blow your own trumpet. You will need plenty of practice and some understanding of what makes an effective presentation. Once you have worked through the practical activities (which include writing, discussing, observing, presenting and providing constructive feedback), you should be able to transform any remaining fear into adrenaline, which, properly channelled, will assist you to perform at your best.

Learning presentation skills

You may well be thinking that not only is it possible to go through life without ever having to speak your mind publicly, but that you will ensure that your career path will not require any such ordeal. This is probably a myth. First, you are unlikely to exercise such control over your career planning (or if you do, you will severely limit your choices), and secondly, you may be called upon or wish to speak your mind in a number of situations outside your career (e.g. attending a public meeting on something you feel strongly about and wanting to put your point of view across). It is not only politicians, actors, teachers, TV personalities or similar public speakers who require good presentation skills. Organisations are realising that people prefer listening to messages rather than reading them. Increasingly employees at all levels are being required to speak to a number of people (either live or via video link). Speaking to a number of people rather than scheduling individual meetings not only saves time but offers greater opportunity for a healthy exchange of views which is likely to be more dynamic than in a series of repeated one-to-one conversations. Knowledge and information is limited unless it is communicated to others. It is worth remembering that as a rule, any audience *wants* the speaker to do a good job. Everyone is uncomfortable when a speaker mumbles, fidgets or forgets what s/he wants to say. Usually your audience wants to hear and understand you. They are silently willing you to do a competent presentation.

A presentation *addresses more than one sense*. Information can be presented orally and visually, through the written word and by means of diagrams. Some areas lend themselves to presentations which employ other senses. A talk on geology might include samples being passed around for the audience to employ their tactile senses. A talk on cooking might include a demonstration where the senses of taste and smell are used. The more senses that are involved in the learning process, the greater the chance that the brain will receive the message. If you ever have an opportunity to get a point across by appealing to other than the usual auditory or visual senses, *use it*!

A presentation is *personal*. The information received by the audience is not limited to what you say or what you show them. A host of other signals are sent unconsciously by your body language.

Presentations are exceptionally *good for explaining concepts*. Ideas can be introduced one at a time through several different senses and built upon to develop a principle. The presenter can encourage the audience to stop him/her and ask questions if any stage is unclear. The presenter can also observe lack of understanding in the faces of the audience and can consequently reiterate certain key points where necessary.

Persuasive argument can be put very effectively through a presentation. This skill is highly valued by some employers. The effectiveness of a persuasive argument can depend to a large extent on the way the talk is structured (see previous chapter).

During a presentation you have a *psychological advantage* because you control the environment. By presenting your case personally to your peers, you have their involvement and with that goes their commitment. If you really want to drive an advantage home, try to bring about a collective decision at your presentation (remembering the ethical issues of rhetoric discussed in Chapters 2 and 3).

Finally a presentation can be entertaining as well as informative. *Introducing humour* can relieve tension but it can back-fire if you, as the presenter, are not completely comfortable with the handling of any potentially humorous material.

Types of presentation

There are many types of presentation from the formal address to a large audience (often with microphone) in which there is little or no opportunity for dialogue to the interactive presentation in which you may choose to engage in some dialogue with your audience. In a formal address or lecture type of talk the presenter usually dominates and little interaction takes place. This sort of address is suitable for large audiences where it would be impractical to invite too many questions. In this setting the presenter needs to structure the material so that a dialogue is set up with an imagined audience, thus engaging the audience in a kind of dialogue where they act as the imagined interlocutor.

An interactive talk or discussion type of presentation, where the presenter sits or stands close to the audience, offers different opportunities. The presenter can pause between sections of the presentation to assess whether the audience has understood everything. Questions and further discussion may ensue at the end of this sort of intimate presentation. For a presentation to be highly interactive, the maximum number in the audience should be about fifteen.

Your talk may fall somewhere between these two extremes. No matter what type of presentation you are intending to give, *you must be able to retain effective control*. If you lose the attention of your audience by being too convoluted or boring or long-winded then you will lose credibility and little or no information will be transmitted. The following role-play activity should demonstrate several pitfalls which will help you to remember what *not* to do.

ACTIVITY 1:

Read the following scripts of presentations (which are either openings to a longer address or complete speeches) aloud. If you are working in groups, take turns to perform them to each other. Think about the effect your speech would probably make on your audience. If you are working in groups, the listeners should take notes on the effect the particular speech is making on them. Jot down some notes after each presentation.

Special reminder to presenters: make sure you follow the instructions, remembering that if you use any visual aids such as overhead transparencies, you should stand in front of them, obscuring them from the maximum number of people in your study group!

- Read your extract aloud (no need to prepare more than a swift glance).
- Do not make any eye contact with your audience (whoever they are).
- Do not pause (imagine you have a train to catch and have to deliver your presentation before you can leave).
- Do not invite any questions.
- Sit down immediately you have finished.

Presentation 1

My presentation today is on the nature of the linguistic sign. Perhaps something has occurred in the history of the concept of structure that could be called an 'event', if this loaded word did entail a meaning which it is precisely the function of structural – or structuralist – thought to reduce or to suspect. I will speak of an 'event', nevertheless, but I shall use quotation marks to serve as a precaution. What would this event be then? Its exterior form would be that of a *rupture* and a redoubling. I shall show you that the concept of structure and even the word structure itself are as old as the *epistémé* and that their roots thrust deep into the soil of ordinary language, into whose deepest recesses the *epistémé* plunges in order to gather them up and to make them part of itself in a metaphorical displacement.

(Benveniste 1987: 77)

Presentation 2

Today I am going to explain about expert system shells. During the early days of expert system applications (such as DENDRAL and MYCIN), expert systems had to be developed in programming language like PROLOG, LISP, or C. However, expert system development software, called shells, are now available. These shells come with an inference engine and several tools that allow the knowledge engineer to design the knowledge database and the end-user interface. I have chosen VP-Expert by Wordtech Systems, Inc. as the expert system shell for use in this presentation because of: a) its English-like rule construction and its built-in editor; b) its ability to exchange data with dBASE compatible database files and ASCII text files; c) its explanation facility; d) its forward and backward chaining inference engine; and e) its affordable cost for the educational version.

(Patankar 1998: 50)

Presentation 3

My presentation today arises out of the number of questions I have received relating to the law. It is a well-established principle that, in the absence of express words or necessary implication, statutes do not bind the Crown. It is the Department's view that, to the extent that staff residences are Crown property (by virtue of the vesting of the freehold in the Security of State), they cannot be designated under section 5 of the 1988 Act. Designation under that section enables a collective community charge to be levied on a person with a qualifying interest in the designation dwelling. So to clarify this further, those with qualifying interests are persons who either have the freehold interest (where there is no single leasehold interest) or have an interest in a lease or under lease which is not itself subject to a single inferior leasehold interest. In the case of properties on which I received most queries, the freehold will be vested in the Crown and it is unlikely that there will be a qualifying leasehold interest. Accordingly, and on the basis that the relevant provisions of the 1988 Act do not bind the Crown, there is unlikely to be any person in relation to those properties who is capable of being subject to a charging authority's collective community charge. This must surely be good news for many of you gathered here today. It would not be appropriate for me to comment on the actions of the community charge registration officer in the absence of details of the particular case in question.

(Plain English Campaign 1994: 42)

Presentation 4

Good afternoon Ladies and Gentlemen. Before the show begins, I would like to introduce you to the history of the art of circus. What is circus, where did it originate and how is it related to other performance arts? The problem of the circus is at first its difficulty to evolve itself. It lives on stereotypes sometimes transforming it from art to simple artisanate. Some people believe that the art of circus belongs to the past and that it is inextricably linked to the traditions and memories of our fathers and grandfathers. They assume that there is no place for modern thinking and experimentation in relation to the circus. No! This is not my view. In fact, this is at the very heart of the question that we need to search for new avenues. This new direction is not only to be found going down the avenue of Centre National des Arts du Cirque but elsewhere too. Here in Potters Bar in 1998 you are about to see the Circus of the Future. Our ground-breaking (if not limb-breaking) feats and earth-shattering spectacles will prove to you forever that the art of circus can and has been elevated to pure art. Ladies and Gentlemen, enjoy!

(Plain English Campaign 1994: 80)

Presentation 5

Hello, my name is ——— and I'm a second-year humanities student. During my first days at university I felt overwhelmed by all the information we were given in packs, by lecturers and on notice boards. All I really wanted to know was: Which are the best pubs? Where is it cheap and cheerful to eat? Which are the best and worst lecturers? And any juicy gossip about anyone at all. Muggins here has been persuaded to share with you my knowledge and experience as someone who has just completed a year in this wonderful institution. Pin your ears back because I'm going to answer all these questions and give you a chance to add any more of your own afterwards. I don't guarantee to be able to answer everything but I can probably point you in the direction of someone who can. Okay, here goes. The Baker's Arms; Valentino's; the Students' Union café for convenience, and Jo's café for variety; Mary Gift O'Gab, Ryan Enigma, John Wingit and Sarah Muddle – in that order. As to the real low-down on student life and the latest gossip, I suggest you meet me in the Tram almost any evening (or lunch time, come to that). For a pint I can wax quite lyrical on most topics. Are there any questions which can't wait until opening time? I doubt it. Good luck; you'll need it!

Analyse why these presentations were effective or ineffective. Think about content and structure, openings and signposting, clarity and explanation of terms, as well as delivery issues such as tone, pitch, pace, pauses, emphasis, body language and other means of capturing your audience (or not). Do not attempt to analyse the speeches on paper, use only the information you heard or saw.

ACTIVITY 2:

Using your exploration of these different examples, now write down a list of five cardinal errors of presentation as if for a book of this kind. Try to give actual examples of such errors from examples you have seen.

Register

In your analysis of the examples of poor presentations you probably noticed that the language was inappropriate in some of the presentations not only because of the convoluted grammatical structures but also because of the use of inappropriate registers. Each extract presented was intended for a specific, and in some cases quite specialised, audience. What was lacking in all the examples of bad practice was a sense of any purposeful communication. How could the presenter establish much, if any purposeful communication using language that alienated his or her listeners?

Knowing what register to use (formal or informal or somewhere in between) depends upon judging your audience and the context in which you are giving your presentation. This will usually require some research. If you are giving an after-dinner speech there will probably be certain expectations about providing some entertainment in the form of stories or jokes. You might even be able to experiment with a quite informal register in parts of the speech. However, if you tried to do this in a more formal situation (say you were giving a financial report to a group of bank managers gathered for a board meeting), the register and conventions of an after-dinner speech (given in the evening when people have been drinking and eating and chatting for some time) would be entirely inappropriate.

Presentation 1 is in a register appropriate to an audience of advanced students of linguistics; the second presentation uses a highly technical register which is aimed at computer programmers. However, neither of the two presentations is likely to work with even the intended audiences because they have been written out in a way that is designed to be read but not delivered. The grammatical structures are too convoluted; the prose is too dense.

In the previous chapter the process of preparing your material was linked to the invention and disposition stages of rhetoric (i.e. finding the arguments or proofs and arranging them into an appropriate structure). Here we are assuming that you have selected a particular case study from the previous chapter and that you have:

- researched your material
- researched your audience
- worked out the structure of your case
- worked on the opening.

ACTIVITY 3:

Go back over the preparatory notes you made for one of the presentations in the last chapter and work specifically on the opening and closing. Write out the first and last few sentences as you think they should be delivered. Think about how you want to close (e.g. with a question, a poem, or a quotation, a challenge, a statistic which relates to your opening, a brief anecdote related to a current event, a summary of your main points, an appeal etc.) and write this out. Remember it is almost always better to give a presentation of this kind without having a script which is fully written out. Knowing your material really well and working from key notes or prompt cards gives a much better final result, but here we are asking you to write out full sentences in order to focus on the kind of language and register you might use in your presentation.

ACTIVITY 4:

Rehearse both opening and closing, and if you are working in groups perform them to your study group. Remember that your opening will dictate the whole tone of your presentation and your close should leave the audience feeling satisfied. After each of you has taken your turn, the others should coach you on your performance. You may refer to the set of example criteria we have included in Appendix 1 for guidance. Those who are coaching should gear their advice to the type of presentation the performer has chosen, i.e. either the small-group presentation style or the speech to the larger audience. What are the differences between the skills needed for each? What worked well? What was less effective and why? Coaches should try to increase both the confidence and the skills of the presenter.

The skills and techniques for making an effective presentation will be covered later in the chapter. Try to complete this rehearsal opening activity before you move on.

ACTIVITY 5:

Ask yourself the following questions and then write up five key points to help you improve your presentation skills.

- Why is it that people feel nervous before giving a presentation?
- What things, specifically, worry you about giving a presentation?
- How likely is it that any of your fears will be realised during a presentation?
- How can nerves affect body language and what can you do to minimise these effects?
- What image should you try to project when you are giving a presentation and how can you achieve it?
- Why is a rehearsal useful and how much of the presentation should you rehearse?
- Can you rehearse it in front of someone else, i.e. a friend or partner?

Overcoming your nerves

Once you have performed one or more of these activities you will realise that everyone is affected by anxiety or nerves which can result in both physical and psychological changes. For instance, you may have experienced the symptoms of sweating, shaking hands and legs, rapid breathing and/or increased heart rate. Some speakers experience anxiety as a nervous stomach.

Don't worry! If you have any of these symptoms before or during a presentation you are normal. Almost everyone experiences some stress before presentations. The trick is to make your excess energy work for you. If you learn to make stress work for you, it can be the fuel for more enthusiastic and dynamic presentations.

The following tips for reducing anxiety assume that you have thoroughly prepared your case (see previous chapter). If you have not prepared your case, you cannot expect to give a good presentation. Applying these tips (or any others) will *not* compensate for neglect of preparation.

- *Visualise*: Imagine walking into a room, being introduced, and delivering your presentation with enthusiasm and clarity. See yourself performing as a confident presenter who is enjoying the performance, fielding questions with confidence and summing up key points within the time allocated. Mentally rehearse this sequence with all the details of your particular situation, and it will help you to focus on what you need to do to be successful.
- *Breathe deeply*: When we are anxious we often 'forget' to breathe properly. Sit up, straight but relaxed, and inhale deeply a few times. (Do not do this too often or unnaturally deeply or you may hyperventilate.)
- *Relax*: Instead of thinking about the tension, relax. As you are breathing deeply and naturally, try to clear your mind of everything except the repetition of 'I am calm and relaxed'. Continue this for a few moments and do not allow yourself to be distracted.
- *Releasing tension*: Some people recommend some unobtrusive isometric exercises just before you stand up to give your presentation. Tighten up all your muscles, starting from your toes and calf muscles, up through your body, finally making a 'fist' of everything. Immediately release all the tension and take a deep breath. Repeat this exercise until you feel the tension start to drain away. Remember, this exercise is to be done quietly and unobtrusively so that no one knows you're relaxing!
- *Move around*: Speakers who stand in one spot and never gesture become tense. Make sure you remember to stretch your muscles. You can do this by taking a few steps, either side-to-side or towards the audience. If you are speaking from a lectern you can move away from it for emphasis.

This movement will help you to release tension but it will also draw your audience into the presentation.

- *Eye contact with the audience*: Try to treat your audience as individuals. Look at people as you speak. Even in a large hall you should be able to single out a few individuals with whom to make eye contact. Not only will this draw in your audience, it will help to relax you because you become less isolated from the audience, and react to their interest in you.

See yourself as others see you

In the last two exercises where you rehearsed your opening and closing you should have had a chance to give a mini-presentation and to coach others by providing them with constructive feedback.

Without realising it, we often reveal a great deal about ourselves by our body language. Some presenters move their arms or hands a great deal, others pace or fiddle with their papers or a piece of jewellery, some appear to be wooden as though they consciously do not want to give away anything by overt body language etc. When you sit in lectures or watch a TV presenter, observe the body language. This way you will become conscious of some of the uses of both effective and ineffective body language.

Use body language carefully

Be aware of how you carry yourself. Whatever your height, learn to walk tall. Poise affects your self-confidence. If you look confident, you portray authority. Visualise a confident speaker and emulate what s/he does. Remember that all body language is a kind of non-verbal communication. Gestures are wonderful but they can be hilariously overdone, particularly by professional speakers. Used in moderation they can help to animate your presentation. If you like making gestures, here are a few observations from experts on body language and gesture:

- Slow, open gestures, palms towards the audience, open arms and open hands give a message which says 'Trust me'.
- Circular, sharing, open-armed movements suggest that 'We're all in this together'.
- Finger movements can be used to enumerate successive points 1, 2, 3 . . . (beware how you indicate point two!). But don't look as though you are ticking off your audience.
- Avoid any brisk, jabbing gestures, or closed fists, or chopping motions. They make the audience angry. There are people who do this deliberately

and then manipulate the audience anger towards some unseen enemy. Arthur Scargill used brisk downward jabbing finger gestures which had the effect of cueing the audience to applaud before he appeared to have finished. This is a clever trick which gives the impression that your audience is erupting with spontaneous enthusiasm. When Stalin used this technique, he took no chances. He stationed KGB guards in the audience to reinforce the enthusiasm. Unless you can be sure of carrying off this sort of coup, avoid all jabbing gestures.

Giving and receiving feedback

Giving and receiving feedback can be a very valuable exercise. But the feedback needs to be constructive and sensitive in order to be effective. An assessor should:

- attempt to remove all personality clashes, likes or dislikes and be impartial
- use language which depersonalises the process
- observe and listen with full concentration
- try to preface potentially hurtful criticisms which might embarrass an overly sensitive presenter with an encouraging comment about something s/he did well
- use his or her knowledge and understanding of the task to help frame any constructive criticism (this also helps to depersonalise your comments)
- ensure that only criticisms which will help the performer are voiced (there is no point telling someone that they are the wrong shape for commanding attention or that their cross-eye is unnerving to the audience!)
- be able to justify and stand by a given mark
- be sufficiently flexible to modify the mark providing adequate contrary evidence is presented.

ACTIVITY 6:

In Activity 4 you should have had a chance to give and receive feedback. Spend about five minutes on your own answering the following questions and writing your answers in two columns headed 'When I receive feedback...' and 'When I give feedback...'.

Receiving feedback (assessment)
- What was the main point made about your presentation that you remember?
- List three criticisms.
- List three good points.
- What comments did you find particularly helpful?
- What comments did you find threatening or uncomfortable (these might be the same as for the previous question)?

- What was your overriding feeling as you were listening to your peers' comments about your performance (e.g. anger, fear, gratitude, interest, defensive etc.)?

Giving feedback (assessment)
- Were you completely honest (albeit tactful) in the feedback you gave your peers?
- If not, why not?
- Do you think your comments will help presenters do better next time?
- If not, why not?
- Can you think of things you should have said and didn't?
- If so, what were they and why did you omit them?

ACTIVITY 7:

If you are working in groups, discuss and compare your answers together.

Draw up a list entitled 'What makes an effective assessor or provider of feedback?'. Once you have done this, compare your list with ours and discuss.

Using anecdotes, analogies and examples

There are no hard and fast rules about how you bring your material to life. This will largely depend on your own personal style and what you feel comfortable with. Anecdotes can be witty or funny, catastrophic or pointless. Only you can decide whether an anecdote will enhance your presentation. Often time constraints will not allow for anecdotes.

Analogies can help to lighten and clarify abstract concepts. They can also be used to help you persuade your audience of your point of view by asking them to consider an analogous situation or by imagining themselves in the shoes of someone else. Examples are useful but be careful you do not use highly complex ones which might allow the audience to lose track of the overall structure and key points of your presentation. Remember that you must keep control of the general direction of your presentation and take your audience with you.

ACTIVITY 8:

Consider what anecdotes, analogies and examples might be used in your presentation. Advice to presenters in business is to keep the message short and simple – the acronym by which they remember this is KISS (Keep It Short and Simple). How can you achieve brevity and simplicity in your presentation? How might you use visual aids, if at all, in this presentation? Are there any other props that might be useful?

Practice makes perfect

There is a great deal of truth in this saying, but if you over-practice the presentation can come across as rather stagey and even dull, especially if you yourself are bored by the material. Practice is useful to control nerves, to make sure that you find the right pace and don't go too fast. If you try out your presentation on a trial audience you will be able to ask them when they need you to explain more, or signpost your points more clearly, or speak more slowly. Another technique is to record your presentation on video or into a tape recorder. This way you can put yourself into the shoes of the audience and answer some of these questions yourself. Churchill practised all his speeches several times, asking his secretary to take notes and provide him with feedback.

Voice control

You don't have to speak with a BBC voice to be a successful presenter. Accents, including very strong regional or foreign accents, can add a great deal of interest to a presentation and may even allow you to keep the audience alert longer. The important factors are clear enunciation, pacing, and modulation of the voice. When you first practise you will probably find that you speak too quickly because of nerves. Try going more slowly than feels quite natural. It should help you to relax more and it will command the audience's attention more effectively. However, a presentation which is given too slowly and with little modulation may begin to sound like a funeral dirge and you may never recapture your audience. Practise what works best for you. Here is some general advice about voice control.

- Vary the pace but never gabble.
- Change the pitch of your voice in appropriate places.
- Dropping to a soft voice in places adds authority.
- Practise reciting a piece in a high pitch, then a low pitch, fast and enthusiastically or slow and solemnly.
- Record your presentation and play it back, listening for pacing, pitch and audibility.

Pause for emphasis

You may think that to stress a particularly important point, you should raise your voice. This is a common error.

- Avoid raising your voice to add emphasis; instead try pausing and intonation.
- Pause . . . it implies that what's coming next is important.
- Whenever a presenter builds in a pause, notice how the audience strains to hear what's coming next.
- Stop completely for up to five seconds just before you make your most important statement.

Use repetition and signposting

Repetition should only be used where you want to emphasise an important point. If you overuse this technique you will irritate your audience, who may feel you are patronising them. Signposting helps to keep the structure of your presentation transparent to all (including you!). At key stages in your presentation you should refer back to what you have covered and where you are going next (e.g. 'Having looked at A and B, I shall now move on to C, in which I shall ask about implications for the future . . .'). Signposting is like a mini-summing up along the way in preparation for your final summing up at the end.

- Only repeat important key points.
- Tell your audience what you are going to say.
- Tell your audience your primary points and overall objective.
- Tell your audience what you have said.

ACTIVITY 9:

Return to your notes on the presentation you began earlier and consider the following questions.

- Where might repetition be useful in this presentation?
- Which points deserve to be prefaced by a pause?
- Where would it be most appropriate to change the pitch?
- How do you monitor the reactions of the audience?
- What signs are you looking for?
- How can you make your voice more interesting?
- How can you make sure that you don't race the material?
- How can you sum up your case effectively at the end?
- What do you want the audience to agree to?

Notes, demonstrations and visual aids

Visual aids or demonstrations of any kind are important in that they help to bring your material to life. Visual material is often what stays in people's minds for longest after a presentation. It can help you to create the right atmosphere so that your audience is intrigued, moved, angered by some alarming statistics, or amused.

In one of the BBC's Royal Institution Christmas Lectures entitled 'Staying Alive: The Body in Balance', the speaker explained the mystery of heat control. One demonstration involved wiring up different parts of the body of a volunteer who then immersed himself in a bath of water which was the temperature of the North Sea. Regular readings were taken from the parts which were submerged and those which remained outside the water, showing how the body redistributes its energy to maximise the chances of survival. Whilst this was a complicated demonstration to set up on stage in front of a live audience, it created a memorable impact. I'll bet that everyone who attended or watched the lecture will remember this particular demonstration and the visible evidence it provided. This is not to suggest that such elaborate demonstrations are necessary or even desirable, but rather to reinforce the importance of using whatever aid is appropriate to engage the interest of your audience, A simple picture, diagram or photo to demonstrate a particular point or illustrate a comparison can be just as effective.

Visual aids chosen with care can help to bring your speech alive. You can use pre-prepared visuals for complex interrelated ideas, persuasive communication or marking a particularly important point which you want the audience to remember.

Don't use over-complicated visuals – everybody in the audience must understand every aid you use by the time you have finished with it. I have been frustrated on a number of occasions where a presenter has used visuals which are too complex to encompass in the time or so dense that only the front two rows have any chance of being able to read them. Here is some general advice about using visual aids.

- Visuals must complement what you say.
- You may wish to have a visual for every point you want your audience to remember.
- Don't use a visual aid you do not need.
- Make sure there are no spelling mistakes.
- Overhead transparencies allow you to write, trace shapes or cartoon figures.
- Use large letters (with a stencil if your hand wobbles).
- Achieve a good balanced layout.
- Use bold colours (but not too many on one visual).

Remember to mark on your cue cards or notes where you intend to use visual aids. If you are sufficiently confident to give a presentation without any notes (because you have prepared so thoroughly) you might find that a few carefully designed overhead transparencies are all you need to trigger your memory.

It is never advisable to work from a complete script when you are giving a presentation. Even if you have written it in a colloquial and speech-based style, it will be immediately apparent to your audience that you are reading all your words. It will also mean that your eyes will be glued to the page and this will undermine your enthusiasm and effectiveness. This is not to say that you shouldn't write out a script if you feel you need to, in a late stage in the preparation, but you should reduce it to key points by the time you give your presentation.

The key points should be reduced still further to single words or phrases (to trigger your memory) which some presenters like to put on cue cards or others write in fairly large print on a single sheet of A4 paper. If you use cue cards you can punch a hole in one corner and tie them together so that you can rotate each card once you have finished with it. (Tying cue cards together avoids the embarrassment of dropping loose cards and having to spend seemingly interminable minutes trying to sort them out in front of your audience.)

Visual aids can help to divert attention away from you. This may help you to relax into your speech but you do not want to lose control of your audience. For this reason, long handouts can be distracting as your audience may flip through them during your presentation, causing distraction to others. One-page handouts can be very useful, however, especially when you have short quotes you want to introduce, as the audience can add notes to the handout and have a record of the presentation to take away with them. Sometimes it is useful to add your main points to the handout too, so the audience can locate themselves within the structure of your presentation if they lose concentration. You can do the same or similar things through using an overhead projector, of course.

Words alone are not visuals: where you do use words, make them provide visual impact by means of graphic devices such as:

- underlining, boxes or circles
- bullets or asterisks
- careful layout
- use of space.

Some final preparations

If you have read the two chapters 'Preparing your case' and 'Presenting your case', and practised the activities, you should know how to set about giving an effective presentation. The following list focuses on what you can do to increase your fluency and build your confidence for the presentation itself.

- Record your speech using only your notes.
- Adjust the material as necessary.
- Ask a friend or relative to listen to your speech and give you feedback (you can give them the criteria sheet in Appendix 1 for guidance).
- Borrow a camcorder and video yourself giving your speech.
- When watching yourself, try to imagine you are hearing the material for the first time – pretend it is someone else giving a presentation.

ACTIVITY 10:

Write some final notes for yourself on what *you* need to work on and remember as you prepare for the presentation itself. Think about all the three parts of the preparation – material, yourself, and audience – as well as about delivery.

Summary

In this chapter we have explored:

- presentation skills
- register and audience
- peer feedback
- overcoming your nerves
- practising
- using anecdotes and examples
- voice control
- notes, demonstrations and visual aids.

References

Benveniste, E. (1987) 'The Nature of the Linguistic Sign' in Rick Rylance (ed.), *Debating Texts: A Reader in Twentieth-Century Literary Theory and Method*. Milton Keynes: Open University Press.

Grigg, J. (1978) *A Biography of Lloyd George*. London. Methuen. Cited in N. Stanton (1982) *The Business of Communicating*. London and Sydney: Pan Books.

Patankar, M. (1998) 'A Rule-Based Expert System Approach to Academic Advising', *Innovations in Education and Training International* 35: 1.

Plain English Campaign (1994) *Utter Drivel! A Decade of Jargon and Gobbledegook*. London: Robson Books.

Wallechinsky, D., Wallace, I. and Wallace, A. (1977) *The Book of Lists*. London: Corgi.

Appendix 1: Sample criteria sheet for peer oral assessment

Date of presentation:
Name of presenter:
Subject of presentation:
Instructions: Each student should complete one assessment sheet for each presentation made by the members of their study group (normally four to six students). These assessment sheets should be completed individually, immediately after the presentation, without consultation with other members of the group. Once completed, these sheets should be handed to the seminar leader, who will use the group's comments and indicated class mark to arrive at the final mark.

CONTENT – You might like to consider the following in your comment:

- evidence of appropriate research
- appropriateness of material for specified audience
- relevance of material for specified task.

ORGANISATION – You might like to consider the following in your comment:

- quality and coherence of argument
- effectiveness of 'signposting'
- effectiveness of introduction and conclusion
- ability to structure content effectively.

DELIVERY – You might like to consider the following in your comment:

- appropriateness of language for specified audience
- delivery (body language, audibility, eye contact)

- planning (pace and keeping to time)
- clarity/intelligibility
- use of notes and other aids
- general effectiveness of contact with audience.

STUDENT SUGGESTED TOTAL CLASSMARK =

Please indicate the *classmark* (not mark) from the following groups: fail (0–39), third (40–49), 2.2 (50–59), lower 2.1 (60–65), upper 2.1 (65–69), first (70 upwards, we rarely give marks over 80).

Appendix 2: Sample practice presentation scenarios

Directions: Choose one of the following tasks and give a five-minute presentation. You will need to be aware of the audience identified in your chosen task and the criteria by which you are being assessed.

1. You are an A-level English teacher working in an English department of a large secondary school which cannot decide on which modern poetry anthology to use for the A-level classes. Your Head of Department has asked you to do some research, choose three suitable anthologies, introduce them to your fellow English teachers and argue the case for the one you think is best.
Make your case.

2. You work for Radio One as a producer/writer. Your boss has suggested a new five-minute current-affairs slot aimed at 20–35-year-olds in which a speaker argues a point of view that relates to the contemporary music scene. She asks you to research, script and present a pilot programme on the subject of, for instance, 'Why pop stars should be allowed to talk about drugs in the media' to be presented to the production team.

3. You are a member of a political lobby group committed to persuading the government to invest more money in workplace nurseries. The group also believes that child-care is an issue relevant to parents and not just mothers. You have been invited to make your case to a government committee looking into national child-care provision. You are told that the committee will also hear a presentation from a right-wing political lobby group who will argue that women should not be encouraged to work full-time because working mothers undermine family life.

4. You are a third-year English Literature student. Your course tutors have asked you to be a student representative on a committee they have set up to make radical changes to the English literature curriculum. They are considering turning the English degree into an intensive twentieth-century studies course, with a large element of film and media studies. You have been asked to consult with fellow students and to present a paper to the Curriculum Committee which represents a range of different student responses to the proposal and to use these to argue for or against the proposed changes.

5. You work for the script-writing team of either *Eastenders*, *Coronation Street* or *Brookside*. You feel that the series needs a new story-line which will address the problem of homelessness amongst young people, but you know the other members of the team will oppose this idea because they do not think the issue is sufficiently important. Make your case to the script-writing team for why you think a major soap should address this issue and suggest how it might do it.

Glossary

Tory Young

adjacency pairs	A term used to describe the pairs of question or statement and response which make up conversations.
anaphoric reference	Reference made to earlier comments or material during a conversation.
back-channel behaviour	Gestures or comments made by listeners during conversation to show that they are processing and understanding what has been said.
claimant	In an argument the party who makes the initial case.
closing implicative	Comments made which indicate that one speaker wishes to bring the conversation to an end (e.g. '*I'd better go now*').
contractions	Words which are usually shortened for ease of speaking (e.g. *it's* for *it is* and *won't* for *will not*).
deictic	Words such as *this*, *those*, *there* which are dependent on context.
deliberative	One of the three main categories of oratory: rhetoric intended to persuade an audience to approve or disapprove of a particular point of view or policy. See *forensic* and *epideictic*.
dialogic/dialogism	Mikhail Bahktin's term for a novel which contains debates which are discussed throughout the novel and continue after its end.
disposition	The arrangement of evidence; identified by Quintillian as one of three key factors in the composition of a persuasive argument. See *invention* and *style*.
elliptical grammatical forms	Incomplete sentences, found in conversations because they are verbal and often informal.

epideictic	One of the three main categories of oratory: rhetoric usually used in a ceremonial context to enlarge on the praiseworthiness or blameworthiness of a person or group. See *deliberative* and *forensic*.
ethos	One of the three main categories defined by Aristotle in his classification of rhetoric, meaning persuasion through personality and stance. See *pathos* and *logos*.
filler/reinforcer words	Words such as *umm*, *er*, *like*, *right* and *sort of* which fill in the pauses while we think as we speak.
forensic	One of the three main categories of oratory: rhetoric intended to achieve condemnation or approval of a person's actions. See *deliberative* and *epideictic*.
framing	In conversation the meaning is signalled by using appropriate tone and body language to aid comprehension and avoid misunderstanding. This is called *framing* the message.
iconic	Iconic gestures are those used during conversation which mimic what they refer to, for instance the size of an object.
interlocuter	In an argument the party who responds or objects to the claimant's position, putting forward counter-claims and producing evidence to support new claims.
invention	The finding of arguments or proofs; identified by Quintillian as one of three key factors in the composition of a persuasive argument. See *disposition* and *style*.
logos	One of the three main categories defined by Aristotle in his classification of rhetoric, meaning persuasion through reasoning. See *ethos* and *pathos*.
metamessage	The total message that is given not just from the meaning of the words that you speak but the context and manner in which they are spoken and your body language at the time.
monologic/ monologism	Bakhtin's term for a novel which does not contain debate or dialogue but favours one dominant way of looking at the world.
pathos	One of the three main categories defined by Aristotle in his classification of rhetoric, meaning persuasion through the arousal of emotion. See *ethos* and *logos*.
register	The variety of language used, relating to purpose and situation.
rhetoric	The 'arts of persuasion', from ancient Greek.
style	The choice of words, verbal patterns and rhythms that will most effectively express the material; identified

by Quintillian as one of the three key factors in the composition of a persuasive argument. See *invention* and *disposition*.

syntax The study of sentence structure, including word structure.

terminal exchange Endings of conversations (e.g. *'Goodbye'*, *'See you soon'*, *'Take care'*).

turn-suppressing and turn-claiming cues The ways we indicate to the person we are talking to that we want to speak, by suggesting with gestures that s/he should give up their turn or that it is our turn.

Further reading

Aijmer, Karin (1996) *Conversational Routines in English: Convention and Creativity*. London: Longman.

Andrews, Richard (1995) *Teaching and Learning Argument*. London: Cassell.

Burke, Peter (1993) *The Art of Conversation*. Cambridge: Polity.

Caplan, Pat (ed.) (1995) *Understanding Disputes: The Politics of Argument*. Oxford: Berg.

Clarke, Stephen and Sinker, John (1992) *Arguments*. Cambridge: Cambridge University Press.

Cockcroft, Robert and Cockcroft, Susan (1992) *Persuading People: An Introduction to Rhetoric*. Basingstoke: Macmillan.

Costello, Patrick J.M. and Mitchell, Sally (eds.) (1995) *Competing and Consensual Voices: The Theory and Practice of Argument*. Clevedon: Multilingual Matters.

Crosswhite, J. (1996) *The Rhetoric of Reason: Writing and the Attractions of Argument*. Madison: University of Wisconsin Press.

Denny, Richard (1994) *Speak for Yourself: Tested Techniques for Improving Your Communication and Presentation Skills*. London: Kogan Page.

Dixon, Peter (1971) *Rhetoric*. London: Methuen.

Graham, Derek (1992) *Presentation Skills*. Knebworth: Spearhead Direct.

Hutton, Jackie and Wainwright, Judith (1992) *Your Own Words*. Walton-on-Thames: Nelson Press.

Langford, David (1994) *Analysing Talk: Investigating Verbal Interaction in English*. Basingstoke: Macmillan.

Mandel, Steve (1989) *Effective Presentation Skills*. London: Kogan Page.

Nash, Walter (1989) *Rhetoric: The Wit of Persuasion*. Oxford: Blackwell.

Rawlins, Karen (1993) *Presentation and Communication skills: A Handbook for Practitioners*. London: Macmillan Magazines.

Stevens, Michael (1987) *Improving Your Presentation Skills: A Complete Action Kit*. London: Kogan Page.

Tannen, Deborah (1998) *The Argument Culture: Changing the Way We Argue and Debate*, with British examples and additions by Michael Leapman. London: Virago.

Tierney, Elizabeth P. (1996) *How To Make Effective Presentations*. Thousand Oaks, CA, and London: Sage Publications.

Vickers, Brian (1988) *In Defence of Rhetoric*. Oxford: Oxford University Press.

Wardhaugh, Ronald (1985) *How Conversation Works*. Oxford: Basil Blackwell.

Ward, Russ (1997) *Logical Argument in the Research Paper*. Fort Worth and London: Harcourt Brace College Publishers.

Yoder, Elmon E. (1996) *Essential Presentation Skills*. Aldershot: Gower.

Index